REACHING OUT

Other Henri J. M. Nouwen titles from Doubleday

AGING

COMPASSION

CREATIVE MINISTRY

THE GENESEE DIARY

THE INNER VOICE OF LOVE

LIFESIGNS

THE RETURN OF THE PRODIGAL SON

THE ROAD TO DAYBREAK

THE WOUNDED HEALER

REACHING OUT

The Three Movements of the Spiritual Life

HENRI J. M. NOUWEN

IMAGE BOOKS
DOUBLEDAY
NEW YORK LONDON TORONTO SYDNEY AUCKLAND

To my mother and father

AN IMAGE BOOK
PUBLISHED BY DOUBLEDAY
a division of Bantam Doubleday Dell Publishing Group, Inc.
1540 Broadway, New York, New York 10036

IMAGE, DOUBLEDAY, and the portrayal of a deer drinking from
a stream are trademarks of Doubleday, a division of Bantam
Doubleday Dell Publishing Group, Inc.

Biblical excerpts from The Jerusalem Bible, copyright
© 1966 by Darton, Longman & Todd, Ltd., and Doubleday.
Used by permission of the publishers.

Excerpt from *The Prophet* by Kahlil Gibran reprinted with
permission of the publisher, Alfred A. Knopf, Inc. Copyright 1923 by
Kahlil Gibran; Renewal copyright 1951 by Administrators C.T.A.
of Kahlil Gibran Estate, and Mary G. Gibran.

DRAWINGS BY MONA MARK

Library of Congress Cataloging-in-Publication Data
Nouwen, Henri J.M.
    Reaching out
    "Complete and unabridged."
    Bibliography: p.
    1. Spiritual life—Catholic authors.   I.Title.
BX2350.2.N676 1986 248.4'82   86-2901
ISBN 0-385-23682-4 (pbk.)

ACKNOWLEDGMENTS

The first plans for this book developed during a short, lively seminar on Christian Spirituality at the Yale Divinity School. Its last pages were written two and a half years later during a long, quiet retreat at the Trappist Abbey of the Genesee. Although this book is closer to me than anything I have written and tries to articulate my most personal thoughts and feelings about being a Christian, it definitively is the book that needed and received the most help.

Without the sincere interest, the critical response and the original contributions of many students, I would never have been able to distinguish between what is personal and what is private, between what is universal and what is "just me."

I am grateful to Gary Cash for his careful assistance in helping me integrate in this text many ideas that were expressed by students as a response to our first seminar. I also am very thankful to Ellie Drury for encouraging me to say what I had to say directly and straightforwardly, and to Mrs. James Angell for helping me say it in correct English.

I owe a special word of thanks to John J. Delaney, Dorothy Holman and John Eudes Bamberger for their invaluable editorial suggestions and to Pat Murray Kelly for her generous and skillful assistance in the typing and retyping of the manuscript.

Acknowledgments

To my mother and father, who created the space where I could hear and follow God's call, I dedicate this book with love and affection.

Abbey of the Genesee
Piffard, New York

CONTENTS

FOREWORD

This book is a response to the question: "What does it mean to live a life in the Spirit of Jesus Christ?" Therefore, it is a personal book, a book born out of struggles which in the first place were and still are my own. But during the years it became more and more clear that by deepening these struggles, by following them to their roots, I was touching a level where they could be shared. This book does not offer answers or solutions but is written in the conviction that the quest for an authentic Christian spirituality is worth the effort and the pain, since in the midst of this quest we can find signs offering hope, courage and confidence.

During the last few years I have read many studies about spirituality and the spiritual life; I have listened to many lectures, spoken with many spiritual guides and visited many religious communities. I have learned much, but the time has come to realize that neither parents nor teachers nor counselors can do much more than offer a free and friendly place where one has to discover his own lonely way. Maybe my own deep-rooted fear to be on my own and alone kept me going from person to person, book to book and school to school, anxiously avoiding the pain of accepting the responsibility for my own life. All that is quite possible, but more important is that the time seems to have come when I can no longer stand back with the remark, "Some say . . . others say," but have to respond to the question, "But what do you say?" (see Mark 8:27-30).

The question about the spiritual life is a very challenging question. It touches the core of life. It forces you to take nothing for granted—neither good nor evil, neither life nor death, neither human beings nor God. That is why this question, while intimately my own, is also the question that asks for so much guidance. That is why the decisions that are most personal ask for the greatest support. That is why, even after many years of education and formation, even after the good advice and counsel of many, I can still say with Dante, "In the middle of the way of our life I find myself in a dark wood."[1] This experience is frightful as well as exhilarating because it is the great experience of being alone, alone in the world, alone before God.

I wanted to write this book because it is my growing conviction that my life belongs to others just as much as it belongs to myself and that what is experienced as most unique often proves to be most solidly embedded in the common condition of being human.

One way to bring all that is written in the following pages together is to say that the spiritual life is a reaching out to our innermost self, to our fellow human beings and to our God. "Reaching out" indeed expresses best the mood and the intention of this book. In the midst of a turbulent, often chaotic, life we are called to reach out, with courageous honesty to our innermost self, with relentless care to our fellow human beings, and with increasing prayer to our God. To do that, however, we have to face and explore directly our inner restlessness, our mixed feelings toward others and our deep-seated suspicions about the absence of God.

For a long time I have been hesitant to write this book, which has such a personal background. How can I tell others about reaching out, while I find myself so often caught in my own passions and weaknesses? I found some consolation and encouragement in the words of one of the most stern ascetics, the seventh-century John of the Ladder, who lived for forty years a solitary life at Mount Sinai. In his chapter on discernment, step 26 of his spiritual ladder, he writes:

> If some are still dominated by their former bad habits, and yet can teach by mere words, let them teach. . . . For perhaps, being put to shame by their own words, they will eventually begin to practice what they teach.[2]

These words seem sufficient to overcome my apprehensions and to make me free to describe the great human call to reach out to God and to those created in his image and likeness.

INTRODUCTION

In a society that gives much value to development, prog-
ress and achievement, the spiritual life becomes quite
easily subject to concerns expressed in questions such as,
"How far advanced am I?"—"Have I matured since I
started on the spiritual path?"—"On what level am I and
how do I move to the next one?"—"When will I reach
the moment of union with God and the experience of
illumination or enlightenment?" Although none of these
questions as such is meaningless, they can become dangerous against the background of a success-oriented society. Many great saints have described their religious
experiences, and many lesser saints have systematized
them into different phases, levels or stages. These distinctions can be helpful for those who write books and
for those who use them to instruct, but it is of great
importance that we leave the world of measurements behind when we speak about the life of the Spirit. A personal reflection can illustrate this:

> When after many years of adult life I ask myself,
> "Where am I as a Christian?" there are just as many
> reasons for pessimism as for optimism. Many of the
> real struggles of twenty years ago are still very much
> alive. I am still searching for inner peace, for creative
> relationships with others and for the experience of
> God, and neither I nor anyone else has any way of
> knowing if the small psychological changes during the

past years have made me a more or a less spiritual man.

We may say, however, one thing: In the middle of all our worries and concerns, often disturbingly similar over the years, we can become more aware of the different poles between which our lives vacillate and are held in tension. These poles offer the context in which we can speak about the spiritual life, because they can be recognized by anyone who is striving to live a life in the Spirit of Jesus Christ.

The first polarity deals with our relationship to ourselves. It is the polarity between loneliness and solitude. The second polarity forms the basis of our relationship to others. This is the polarity between hostility and hospitality. The third, final and most important polarity structures our relationship with God. This is the polarity between illusion and prayer. During our life we become more aware not only of our crying loneliness but also of our real desire for a solitude of the heart; we come to the painful realization not only of our cruel hostilities but also of our hope to receive our fellow humans with unconditional hospitality; and underneath all of this we discover not only the endless illusions which make us act as if we are masters of our fate but also the precarious gift of prayer hidden in the depth of our innermost self. Thus, the spiritual life is that constant movement between the poles of loneliness and solitude, hostility and hospitality, illusion and prayer. The more we come to the painful confession of our loneliness, hostilities and illusions, the more we are able to see solitude, hospitality and prayer as part of the vision of our life. Although after many years of living we often feel more lonely, hostile and filled with illusions than when we had hardly a past to reflect upon, we also know better than before that all these pains have deepened and sharpened our urge to reach out to a solitary, hospitable and prayerful mode of existence.

And so, writing about the spiritual life is like making prints from negatives. Maybe it is exactly the experience of loneliness that allows us to describe the first tentative lines of solitude. Maybe it is precisely the shocking confrontation with our hostile self that gives us words to speak about hospitality as a real option, and maybe we will never find the courage to speak about prayer as a human vocation without the disturbing discovery of our own illusions. Often it is the dark forest that makes us speak about the open field. Frequently prison makes us think about freedom, hunger helps us to appreciate food, and war gives us words for peace. Not seldom are our visions of the future born out of the sufferings of the present and our hope for others out of our own despair. Only few "happy endings" make us happy, but often someone's careful and honest articulation of the ambiguities, uncertainties and painful conditions of life gives us new hope. The paradox is indeed that new life is born out of the pains of the old.

The life of Jesus has made it very clear to us that the spiritual life does not allow by-passes. By-passing loneliness, hostility or illusion will never lead us to solitude, hospitality and prayer. We will never know for sure if we will fully realize the new life that we can discover in the midst of the old. Maybe we will die lonely and hostile, taking our illusions with us in our grave. Many seem to do so. But when Jesus asks us to take up our cross and follow him (Mark 8:34) we are invited to reach out far beyond our broken and sinful condition and give shape to a life that intimates the great things that are prepared for us.

Because of the conviction that to live a spiritual life

means first of all to come to the awareness of the inner polarities between which we are held in tension, this book is divided into three parts, each one representing a different movement of the spiritual life. The first movement, from loneliness to solitude, focuses primarily on the spiritual life as it relates to the experience of our own selves. The second movement, from hostility to hospitality, deals with our spiritual life as a life for others. The third and final movement, from illusion to prayer, offers some tentative formulations of that most precious and mysterious relationship which is the source of all spiritual life, our relationship to God.

It hardly needs to be stressed that these movements are not clearly separated. Certain themes recur in the different movements in various tonalities and often flow into one another as the different movements of a symphony. But hopefully the distinctions will help us better to recognize the different elements of the spiritual life and so encourage us to reach out to our innermost self, our fellow human beings and our God.

REACHING OUT TO OUR INNERMOST SELF

The First Movement:
From Loneliness to Solitude

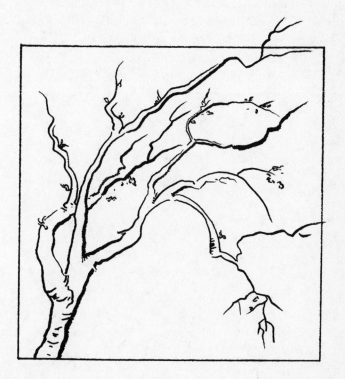

Chapter 1

A SUFFOCATING LONELINESS

———————⟶✢✢⟵———————

Between Competition and Togetherness

It is far from easy to enter into the painful experience of
loneliness. You like to stay away from it. Still it is an
experience that enters into everyone's life at some point.
You might have felt it as a little child when your classmates laughed at you because you were cross-eyed or as
a teen-ager when you were the last one chosen on the
baseball team. You might have felt it when you were
homesick in a boarding school or angry about non-sense
rules which you could not change. You might have felt it
as a young adult in a university where everyone talked
about grades but where a good friend was hard to find,
or in an action group where nobody paid any attention to
your suggestions. You might have felt it as a teacher
when students did not respond to your carefully prepared lectures or as a preacher when people were dozing
during your well-intentioned sermons. And you still
might feel it day after day during staff meetings, conferences, counseling sessions, during long office hours or
monotonous manual labor, or just when you are by
yourself staring away from a book that cannot keep your
attention. Practically every human being can recall simi-

lar or much more dramatic situations in which he or she has experienced that strange inner gnawing, that mental hunger, that unsettling unrest that makes us say, "I feel lonely."

Loneliness is one of the most universal human experiences, but our contemporary Western society has heightened the awareness of our loneliness to an unusual degree.

During a recent visit to New York City, I wrote the following note to myself:

> Sitting in the subway, I am surrounded by silent people hidden behind their newspapers or staring away in the world of their own fantasies. Nobody speaks with a stranger, and a patroling policeman keeps reminding me that people are not out to help each other. But when my eyes wander over the walls of the train covered with invitations to buy more or new products, I see young, beautiful people enjoying each other in a gentle embrace, playful men and women smiling at each other in fast sailboats, proud explorers on horseback encouraging each other to take brave risks, fearless children dancing on a sunny beach, and charming girls always ready to serve me in airplanes and ocean liners. While the subway train runs from one dark tunnel into the other and I am nervously aware where I keep my money, the words and images decorating my fearful world speak about love, gentleness, tenderness and about a joyful togetherness of spontaneous people.

The contemporary society in which we find ourselves makes us acutely aware of our loneliness. We become increasingly aware that we are living in a world where even the most intimate relationships have become part of competition and rivalry.

Pornography seems one of the logical results. It is intimacy for sale. In the many "porno shops" hundreds of lonely young and old men, full of fear that anyone will recognize them, gaze silently at the pictures of nude girls drawing their minds into intimate close rooms where some stranger will melt away their loneliness. The streets meanwhile shout about the cruel struggle for survival and even the porno corners cannot silence that noise, certainly not when the shop owners keep reminding their customers that they should buy instead of "just looking."

Loneliness is one of the most universal sources of human suffering today. Psychiatrists and clinical psychologists speak about it as the most frequently expressed complaint and the root not only of an increasing number of suicides but also of alcoholism, drug use, different psychosomatic symptoms—such as, headaches, stomach and low-back pains—and of a large number of traffic accidents. Children, adolescents, adults and old people are in growing degree exposed to the contagious disease of loneliness in a world in which a competitive individualism tries to reconcile itself with a culture that speaks about togetherness, unity and community as the ideals to strive for.

Why is it, that many parties and friendly get-togethers leave us so empty and sad? Maybe even there the deep-seated and often unconscious competition between people prevents them from revealing themselves to each other and from establishing relationships that last longer than the party itself. Where we are always welcome, our absence won't matter that much either and when everyone can come, nobody will be particularly missed. Usually there is food enough and people enough willing to eat it, but often it seems that the food has lost the power

to create community and not seldom do we leave the
party more aware of our loneliness than when we came.

The language we use suggests anything but loneliness.
"Please come in, it is so good to see you . . . Let me
introduce you to this very special friend of mine, who
will love to meet you . . . I have heard so much about
you and I can't say how pleased I am to see you now in
person . . . What you are saying is most interesting, I
wish more people could hear that . . . It was so great to
talk to you and to have a chance to visit with you . . . I
dearly hope we will meet again. Know that you are always welcome and don't hesitate to bring a friend . . .
Come back soon." It is a language that reveals the desire
to be close and receptive but that in our society sadly
fails to heal the pains of our loneliness, because the real
pain is felt where we can hardly allow anyone to enter.

The roots of loneliness are very deep and cannot be
touched by optimistic advertisement, substitute love images or social togetherness. They find their food in the
suspicion that there is no one who cares and offers love
without conditions, and no place where we can be vulnerable without being used. The many small rejections
of everyday—a sarcastic smile, a flippant remark, a brisk
denial or a bitter silence—may all be quite innocent and
hardly worth our attention if they did not constantly
arouse our basic human fear of being left totally alone
with "darkness . . . [as our] one companion left"
(Psalm 88).

The Avoidance of the Painful Void

It is this most basic human loneliness that threatens us
and is so hard to face. Too often we will do everything
possible to avoid the confrontation with the experience
of being alone, and sometimes we are able to create the

most ingenious devices to prevent ourselves from being reminded of this condition. Our culture has become most sophisticated in the avoidance of pain, not only our physical pain but our emotional and mental pain as well. We not only bury our dead as if they were still alive, but we also bury our pains as if they were not really there. We have become so used to this state of anesthesia, that we panic when there is nothing or nobody left to distract us. When we have no project to finish, no friend to visit, no book to read, no television to watch or no record to play, and when we are left all alone by ourselves we are brought so close to the revelation of our basic human aloneness and are so afraid of experiencing an all-pervasive sense of loneliness that we will do anything to get busy again and continue the game which makes us believe that everything is fine after all. John Lennon says: "Feel your own pain," but how hard that is!

In 1973 the Educational Television Network showed a series of life portraits of a family in Santa Barbara, California. This series, which was produced under the name "An American Family," offered an honest and candid portrayal of the day-to-day life of Mr. and Mrs. Loud and their five children. Although the revelations about this "average family," which included the divorce of the parents and the homosexual life of the oldest son, shocked many viewers, a detailed film analysis of any family probably would have been as shocking as this one. The film, which was made with the full permission and knowledge of all the members of the family, not only unmasked the illusion that this family could be presented as an example to the American people, but also showed in painful details our tendency to avoid the experience of pain at all costs. Painful issues remained unmentioned and embarrassing situations were simply denied. Pat, the wife and mother in the family, expressed this attitude best when she said, "I don't like things that make me feel uncomfortable." The consequences of this pain-avoidance, however, were well expressed by her eighteen-year-old son when he said, "You see seven lonely people trying desperately to love each other—and not succeeding."[1]

It is not very difficult to see that the Loud family is indeed no exception and in many respects "average" in a society growingly populated with lonely people desperately trying to love each other without succeeding. Is this not in large part due to our inability to face the pain of our loneliness? By running away from our loneliness and by trying to distract ourselves with people and special experiences, we do not realistically deal with our human predicament. We are in danger of becoming unhappy people suffering from many unsatisfied cravings and tortured by desires and expectations that never can be fulfilled. Does not all creativity ask for a certain encounter with our loneliness, and does not the fear of this encounter severely limit our possible self expression?

When I have to write an article and face a white empty sheet of paper I nearly have to tie myself to the chair to keep from consulting one more book before putting my own words on paper. When, after a busy day, I am alone and free I have to fight the urge to make one more phone call, one more trip to the mailbox or one more visit to friends who will entertain me for the last few hours of the day. And when I think about the busy day I sometimes wonder if the educational enterprise so filled with lectures, seminars, conferences, requirements to make up and to fulfill, papers to write and to read, examinations to undergo and to go to, has, in fact, not become one big distraction—once in a while entertaining—but mostly preventing me from facing my lonely self which should be my first source of search and research.

The superficial life to which this leads is vividly portrayed by Henry David Thoreau when he writes:

When our life ceases to be inward and private, conversation degenerates into mere gossip. We rarely meet a man who can tell us any news which he has not read in a newspaper, or been told by his neighbor; and, for the most part, the only difference between us and our fellow is that he has seen the newspaper, or been out to tea, and we have not. In proportion as our inward life fails, we go more constantly and desperately to the post office. You may depend on it, that the poor fellow who walks away with the greatest number of letters proud of his extensive correspondence has not heard from himself this long while.[2]

The first task of any school should be to protect its privilege of offering free time—the Latin word *schola* means free time—to understand ourselves and our world a little better. It really is a hard struggle to keep free time truly free and to prevent education from degenerating into just another form of competition and rivalry.

The problem, however, is that we not only want our freedom but also fear it. It is this fear that makes us so intolerant toward our own loneliness and makes us grab prematurely for what seem to be "final solutions."

The Danger of the Final Solution

There is much mental suffering in our world. But some of it is suffering for the wrong reason because it is born out of the false expectation that we are called to take each other's loneliness away. When our loneliness drives us away from ourselves into the arms of our companions in life, we are, in fact, driving ourselves into excruciating relationships, tiring friendships and suffocating embraces. To wait for moments or places where no pain exists, no separation is felt and where all human restlessness has turned into inner peace is waiting for a dreamworld. No friend or lover, no husband or wife, no community or commune will be able to put to rest our deepest cravings for unity and wholeness. And by burdening others with these divine expectations, of which we ourselves are often only partially aware, we might inhibit the expression of free friendship and love and evoke instead feelings of inadequacy and weakness. Friendship and love cannot develop in the form of an anxious clinging to each other. They ask for gentle fearless space in which we can move to and from each other. As long as our loneliness brings us together with the hope that together we no longer will be alone, we castigate each other with our unfulfilled and unrealistic desires for oneness, inner tranquility and the uninterrupted experience of communion.

It is sad to see how sometimes people suffering from loneliness, often deepened by the lack of affection in their intimate family circle, search for a final solution for their pains and look at a new friend, a new lover or a new community with Messianic expectations. Although their mind knows about their self-deceit, their hearts keep saying, "Maybe this time I have found what I have knowingly or unknowingly been searching for." It is indeed amazing at first sight that men and women who have had such distressing relationships with their parents, brothers or sisters can throw themselves blindly into relationships with far-reaching consequences in the hope that from now on things will be totally different. But we might wonder if the many conflicts and quarrels, the many accusations and recriminations, the many moments of expressed and repressed anger and of confessed or unconfessed jealousies, which are so often part of these rushed-into relationships, do not find their roots in the false claim that the one has to take the other's loneliness away. Indeed, it seems that the desire for "final solutions" often forms the basis for the destructive violence that enters into the intimacy of human encounters. Mostly this violence is a violence of thoughts, violating the mind with suspicion, inner gossip or revengeful fantasies. Sometimes it is a violence of words disturbing the peace with reproaches and complaints, and once in a while it takes the dangerous form of harmful actions. Violence in human relationship is so utterly destructive because it not only harms the other but also drives the self into a vicious circle asking for more and more when less and less is received.

In a time with strong emphasis on interpersonal sensitivity, in which we are encouraged to explore our communicative capacities and experiment with many forms of physical, mental and emotional contact, we are sometimes tempted to believe that our feelings of loneliness and sadness are only a sign of lack of mutual openness. Sometimes this is true and many sensitivity centers make invaluable contributions to the broadening of the range of human interactions. But real openness to each other also means a real closedness, because only he who can hold a secret can safely share his knowledge. When we do not protect with great care our own inner mystery, we will never be able to form community. It is this inner mystery that attracts us to each other and allows us to establish friendship and develop lasting relationships of love. An intimate relationship between people not only asks for mutual openness but also for mutual respectful protection of each other's uniqueness.

Together, Yet Not Too Near

There is a false form of honesty that suggests that nothing should remain hidden and that everything should be said, expressed and communicated. This honesty can be very harmful, and if it does not harm, it at least makes the relationship flat, superficial, empty and often very boring. When we try to shake off our loneliness by creating a milieu without limiting boundaries, we may become entangled in a stagnating closeness. It is our vocation to prevent the harmful exposure of our inner sanctuary, not only for our own protection but also as a service to our fellow human beings with whom we want to enter in a creative communion. Just as words lose their power when they are not born out of silence, so openness loses its meaning when there is no ability to be closed. Our world is full of empty chatter, easy confessions, hollow talk, senseless compliments, poor praise, and boring confidentialities. Not a few magazines become wealthy by suggesting that they are able to furnish us with the most secret and intimate details of the lives of people we always wanted to know more about. In fact, they present us with the most boring trivialities and the most supercilious idiosyncrasies of people whose lives are already flattened out by morbid exhibitionism.

The American way of life tends to be suspicious toward closedness.

When I came to this country for the first time, I was struck by the open-door life style. In schools, institutes and office buildings everyone worked with open doors. I could see the secretaries typing behind their machines, the teachers teaching behind their lecterns, the administrators administering behind their desks and the occasional readers reading behind their books. It seemed as if everyone was saying to me, "Do not hesitate to walk in and interrupt at any time," and most conversations had the same open quality—giving me the impression that people had no secrets and were ready for any question ranging from their financial status to their sex life.

It is clear that most of these are first impressions and that second and third impressions reveal quickly that there is less openness than suggested. But still, closed doors are not popular, and it needs special effort to establish boundaries that protect the mystery of our lives. Certainly in a period of history in which we have become so acutely aware of our alienation in its different manifestations, it has become difficult to unmask the illusion that the final solution for our experience of loneliness is to be found in human togetherness. It is easy to see how many marriages are suffering from this illusion. Often they are started with the hope of a union that can dispel all painful feelings of "not belonging" and continue with the desperate struggle to reach a perfect physical and psychological harmony. Many people find it very hard to appreciate a certain closedness in a marriage and do not know how to create the boundaries that allow intimacy to become an always new and surprising discovery of each other. Still, the desire for protective boundaries by which man and woman do not have to cling to each other, but can move graciously in and out of each other's life circle, is clear from the many times that Kahlil Gibran's words are quoted at a wedding ceremony:

> Sing and dance together and be joyous,
> but let each one of you be alone.
> Even as the strings of a lute are alone
> though they quiver with the same music.

Stand together yet not too near together
For the pillars of the temple stand apart,
and the oak tree and the cypress
grow not in each other's shadow.[3]

From Desert to Garden

[But what then can we do with our essential aloneness
which so often breaks into our consciousness as the experience of a desperate sense of loneliness?]What does it
mean to say that neither friendship nor love, neither
marriage nor community can take that loneliness away?
Sometimes illusions are more livable than realities, and
why not follow our desire to cry out in loneliness and
search for someone whom we can embrace and in whose
arms our tense body and mind can find a moment of
deep rest and enjoy the momentary experience of being
understood and accepted? These are hard questions because they come forth out of our wounded hearts, but
they have to be listened to even when they lead to a
difficult road. This difficult road is the road of conversion, the conversion from loneliness into solitude. Instead of running away from our loneliness and trying to
forget or deny it, we have to protect it and turn it into a
fruitful solitude. To live a spiritual life we must first find
the courage to enter into the desert of our loneliness and
to change it by gentle and persistent efforts into a garden
of solitude. This requires not only courage but also a
strong faith. As hard as it is to believe that the dry deso-
late desert can yield endless varieties of flowers, it is
equally hard to imagine that our loneliness is hiding unknown beauty. The movement from loneliness to solitude, however, is the beginning of any spiritual life because it is the movement from the restless senses to the
restful spirit, from the outward-reaching cravings to the

inward-reaching search, from the fearful clinging to the fearless play.

A young student reflecting on his own experience wrote recently:

When loneliness is haunting me with its possibility of being a threshold instead of a dead end, a new creation instead of a grave, a meeting place instead of an abyss, then time loses its desperate clutch on me. Then I no longer have to live in a frenzy of activity, overwhelmed and afraid for the missed opportunity.

It is far from easy to believe that this is true. Often we go to good men and women with our problems in the secret hope that they will take our burden away from us and free us from our loneliness. Frequently the temporary relief they offer only leads to a stronger recurrence of the same pains when we are again by ourselves. But sometimes we meet and hear that exceptional person who says: "Do not run, but be quiet and silent. Listen attentively to your own struggle. The answer to your question is hidden in your own heart."

In the beautiful book *Zen Flesh, Zen Bones* we find the story of such an encounter.

Daiju visited the master Baso in China. Baso asked: "What do you seek?"

"Enlightment," replied Daiju.

"You have your own treasure house. Why do you search outside?" Baso asked.

Daiju inquired: "Where is my treasure house?"

Baso answered: "What you are asking *is* your treasure house."

Daiju was enlightened! Ever after he urged his friends: "Open your own treasure house and use those treasures."[4]

The real spiritual guide is the one who, instead of advising us what to do or to whom to go, offers us a chance to stay alone and take the risk of entering into our own experience. He makes us see that pouring little bits of water on our dry land does not help, but that we will find a living well if we reach deep enough under the surface of our complaints.

A friend once wrote: "Learning to weep, learning to keep vigil, learning to wait for the dawn. Perhaps this is what it means to be human." It is hard to really believe this because we constantly find ourselves clinging to people, books, events, experiences, projects and plans, secretly hoping that this time it will be different. We keep experimenting with many types of anesthetics, we keep finding "psychic numbing" often more agreeable than the sharpening of our inner sensitivities. But . . . we can at least remind ourselves of our self-deceit and confess at times our morbid predilection for dead-end streets.

The few times, however, that we do obey our severe masters and listen carefully to our restless hearts, we may start to sense that in the midst of our sadness there is joy, that in the midst of our fears there is peace, that in the midst of our greediness there is the possibility of compassion and that indeed in the midst of our irking loneliness we can find the beginnings of a quiet solitude.

Chapter 2

A RECEPTIVE SOLITUDE

―――――――⟫⊹⊹⟪――――――――

Solitude of Heart

The word solitude can be misleading. It suggests being alone by yourself in an isolated place. When we think about solitaries, our mind easily evokes images of monks or hermits who live in remote places secluded from the noise of the busy world. In fact, the words solitude and solitary are derived from the Latin word *solus*, which means alone, and during the ages many men and women who wanted to live a spiritual life withdrew to remote places—deserts, mountains or deep forests—to live the life of a recluse.

It is probably difficult, if not impossible, to move from loneliness to solitude without any form of withdrawal from a distracting world, and therefore it is understandable that those who seriously try to develop their spiritual life are attracted to places and situations where they can be alone, sometimes for a limited period of time, sometimes more or less permanently. But the solitude that really counts is the solitude of heart; it is an inner quality or attitude that does not depend on physical isolation. On occasion this isolation is necessary to develop this solitude of heart, but it would be sad if we considered this essential aspect of the spiritual life as a privilege of monks and hermits. It seems more important than ever to stress that solitude is one of the human capacities that can exist, be maintained and developed in the center of a big city, in the middle of a large crowd and in the context of a very active and productive life. A man or woman who has developed this solitude of heart is no longer pulled apart by the most divergent stimuli of the surrounding world but is able to perceive and understand this world from a quiet inner center.

By attentive living we can learn the difference between being present in loneliness and being present in solitude. When you are alone in an office, a house or an empty waiting room, you can suffer from restless loneliness but also enjoy a quiet solitude. When you are teaching in a classroom, listening to a lecture, watching a movie or chatting at a "happy hour," you can have the unhappy feeling of loneliness but also the deep contentment of someone who speaks, listens and watches from the tranquil center of his solitude. It is not too difficult to distinguish between the restless and the restful, between the driven and the free, between the lonely and the solitary in our surroundings. When we live with a solitude of heart, we can listen with attention to the words and the worlds of others, but when we are driven by loneliness, we tend to select just those remarks and events that bring immediate satisfaction to our own craving needs.

Our world, however, is not divided between lonely people and solitaries. We constantly fluctuate between these poles and differ from hour to hour, day to day, week to week and year to year. We must confess that we have only a very limited influence on this fluctuation. Too many known and unknown factors play roles in the balance of our inner life. But when we are able to recognize the poles between which we move and develop a sensitivity for this inner field of tension, then we no longer have to feel lost and can begin to discern the direction in which we want to move.

The Beginning of the Spiritual Life

The development of this inner sensitivity is the beginning of a spiritual life. It seems that the emphasis on interpersonal sensitivity has at times made us forget to develop the sensitivity that helps us to listen to our own inner voices. Sometimes one wonders if the fact that so many people ask support, advice and counsel from so many other people is not, in large part, due to their having lost contact with their innermost self. They ask: Should I go to school or look for a job, should I become a doctor or a lawyer, should I marry or remain single, should I leave my position or stay where I am, should I go into the military or refuse to go to war, should I obey my superior or follow my own inclination, should I live a poor life or gain more money for the costly education of my children? There are not enough counselors in the world to help with all these hard questions, and sometimes one feels as if one half of the world is asking advice of the other half while both sides are sitting in the same darkness.

On the other hand, when our insecurity does not lead us to others for help, how often does it lead us against others in self-defense? Sometimes it seems that gossip, condemnation of other people's behavior and outright attacks against their life choices are more a sign of our own self-doubt than of our solidly grounded convictions.

Maybe the most important advice to all searching people is the advice that Rainer Maria Rilke gave to the

young man who asked him if he should become a poet.
Rilke says:

> You ask whether your verses are good. You ask me.
> You have asked others before. You send them to maga-
> zines. You compare them with other poems, and you
> are disturbed when certain editors reject your efforts.
> Now . . . I beg you to give up all that. You are look-
> ing outward and that above all you should not do now.
> Nobody can counsel and help you, nobody. There is
> only one single way. Go into yourself. Search for the
> reason that bids you to write; find out whether it is
> spreading out its roots in the deepest places of your
> heart, acknowledge to yourself whether you would
> have to die if it were denied you to write. This above
> all—ask yourself in the stillest hour of your night: *must*
> I write? Delve into yourself for a deep answer. And if
> this should be affirmative, if you may meet this earnest
> question with a strong and simple *"I must,"* then build
> your life according to this necessity; your life even into
> its most indifferent and slightest hour must be a sign
> of this urge and a testimony to it.[1]

To Live the Question

By slowly converting our loneliness into a deep solitude, we create that precious space where we can discover the voice telling us about our inner necessity—that
is, our vocation. Unless our questions, problems and concerns are tested and matured in solitude, it is not realistic
to expect answers that are really our own. How many
people can claim their ideas, opinions and viewpoints as
their own? Sometimes intellectual conversations boil
down to the capacity to quote the right authority at the
right time. Even the most intimate concerns, such as the

concerns about the meaning and value of life and death, can become victims of the fashion of the time. Frequently, we are restlessly looking for answers, going from door to door, from book to book, or from school to school, without having really listened carefully and attentively to the questions. Rilke says to the young poet:

> I want to beg you as much as I can . . . to be patient toward all that is unsolved in your heart and to try to love the questions themselves. . . . Do not now seek answers which cannot be given you because you would not be able to live them. And the point is to live everything. *Live* the questions now. Perhaps you will then gradually, without noticing it, live along some distant day into the answer . . . take whatever comes with great trust, and if only it comes out of your own will, out of some need of your innermost being, take it upon yourself and hate nothing.[2]

This is a very difficult task, because in our world we are constantly pulled away from our innermost self and encouraged to look for answers instead of listening to the questions. A lonely person has no inner time nor inner rest to wait and listen. He wants answers and wants them here and now. But in solitude we can pay attention to our inner self. This has nothing to do with egocentrism or unhealthy introspection because, in the words of Rilke, "what is going on in your innermost being is worthy of your whole love."[3] In solitude we can become present to ourselves. There we can live, as Anne Morrow Lindbergh says, "like a child or a saint in the immediacy of here and now."[4] There "every day, every act is an island, washed by time and space and has an island's completion."[5] There we also can become present to others by reaching out to them, not greedy for attention and affection but offering our own selves to help build a community of love. Solitude does not pull us away from our fellow human beings but instead makes real fellowship possible. Few people have expressed this better than the Trappist monk Thomas Merton, who spent the last years of his life living as a hermit but whose contemplative solitude brought him into very intimate contact with others. On January 12, 1950, he wrote in his diary:

It is in deep solitude that I find the gentleness with which I can truly love my brothers. The more solitary I am, the more affection I have for them. It is pure affection and filled with reverence for the solitude of others.[6]

As his life grew in spiritual maturity, Merton came to see with a penetrating clarity that solitude did not separate him from his contemporaries but instead brought him into a deep communion with them. How powerful this insight was for Merton himself is evident from the moving passage he wrote after a short visit to Louisville where he had watched the people in a busy shopping district. He writes:

. . . though "out of the world" we [monks] are in the same world as everybody else, the world of the bomb, the world of race hatred, the world of technology, the world of mass media, big business, revolution, and all the rest. We take a different attitude to all these things, for we belong to God. Yet so does everybody else belong to God. . . . This sense of liberation from an illusory difference was such a relief and such a joy to me that I almost laughed out loud. And I suppose my happiness could have taken form in these words: "Thank God, thank God that I *am* like other men, that I am only a man among others." . . . It is a glorious destiny to be a member of the human race, though it is a race dedicated to many absurdities and one which makes many terrible mistakes: yet, with all that, God Himself gloried in becoming a member of the human race! To think that such a commonplace realization should suddenly seem like news that one holds the winning ticket in a cosmic sweepstake.

I have the immense joy of being *man*, a member of a race in which God Himself became incarnate. As if the sorrows and stupidities of the human condition could overwhelm me, now I realize what we all are. And if only everybody could realize this! But it cannot be explained. There is no way of telling people that they are walking around shining like the sun.

This changes nothing in the sense and value of my solitude, for it is in fact the function of solitude to make one realize such things with a clarity that would be impossible to anyone completely immersed in the other cares, the other illusions, and all the automatisms of a highly collective existence. My solitude, however, is not my own, for I see now how much it belongs to them—and that I have a responsibility for it in their regard, not just in my own. It is because I am one with them that I owe it to them to be alone, and when I am alone, they are not "they" but my own self. There are not strangers![7]

His own personal experience taught Merton that solitude not only deepens our affection for others but also is the place where real community becomes possible. Although Merton himself lived as a monk first in a monastic community and later in a hermitage, it is clear from this and other writings that what really counts for him is not the physical solitude but the solitude of the heart.

Without the solitude of heart, the intimacy of friendship, marriage and community life cannot be creative.

Without the solitude of heart, our relationships with others easily become needy and greedy, sticky and clinging, dependent and sentimental, exploitative and parasitic, because without the solitude of heart we cannot experience the others as different from ourselves but only as people who can be used for the fulfillment of our own, often hidden, needs.

The mystery of love is that it protects and respects the aloneness of the other and creates the free space where he can convert his loneliness into a solitude that can be shared. In this solitude we can strengthen each other by mutual respect, by careful consideration of each other's individuality, by an obedient distance from each other's privacy and by a reverent understanding of the sacredness of the human heart. In this solitude we encourage each other to enter into the silence of our innermost being and discover there the voice that calls us beyond the limits of human togetherness to a new communion. In this solitude we can slowly become aware of a presence of him who embraces friends and lovers and offers us the freedom to love each other, because he loved us first (see 1 John 4:19).

Holy Ground

All this might sound like a new sort of romanticism, but our own very concrete experiences and observations will help us to recognize this as realism. Often we must confess that the experience of our loneliness is stronger than that of our solitude and that our words about solitude are spoken out of the painful silence of loneliness. But there are happy moments of direct knowing, affirming our hopes and encouraging us in our search for that deep solitude where we can sense an inner unity and live in union with our fellow human beings and our God.

I vividly remember the day on which a man who had been a student in one of my courses came back to the school and entered my room with the disarming remark: "I have no problems this time, no questions to ask you. I do not need counsel or advice, but I simply want to celebrate some time with you." We sat on the ground facing each other and talked a little about what life had been for us in the last year, about our work, our common friends, and about the restlessness of our hearts. Then slowly as the minutes passed by we became silent. Not an embarrassing silence but a silence that could bring us closer together than the many small and big events of the last year. We would hear a few cars pass and the noise of someone who was emptying a trash can somewhere. But that did not hurt. The silence which grew between us was warm, gentle and vibrant. Once in a while we looked at each other with the beginning of a smile pushing away the last remnants of fear and suspicion. It seemed that while the silence grew deeper around us we became more and more aware of a presence embracing both of us. Then he said, "It is good to be here" and I said, "Yes, it is good to be together again," and after that we were silent again for a long period. And as a deep peace filled the empty space between us he said hesitantly, "When I look at you it is as if I am in the presence of Christ." I did not feel startled, surprised or in need of protesting, but I could only say, "It is the Christ in you, who recognizes the Christ in me." "Yes," he said, "He indeed is in our midst," and then he spoke the words which entered into my soul as the most healing words I had heard in many years, "From now on, wherever you go, or wherever I go, all the ground between us will be holy ground." And when he left I knew that he had revealed to me what community really means.

Community as an Inner Quality

This experience explains what Rainer Maria Rilke meant when he said, "Love . . . consists in this, that two solitudes protect and border and salute each other"[8] and what Anne Morrow Lindbergh had in mind when she wrote, "I feel we are all islands in a common sea."[9] It made me see that the togetherness of friends and lovers can become moments in which we can enter into a common solitude which is not restricted by time and place. How often don't we dream about being together with friends without realizing that our dreams are searching for much more than any factual reunion will ever be able to realize? But slowly we can become aware of the possibility of making our human encounters into moments by which our solitude grows and expands itself to embrace more and more people into the community of our life. It indeed is possible for all those with whom we stayed for a long time or for only a moment to become members of that community since, by their encounter in love, all the ground between them and us has indeed become holy ground, and those who leave can stay in the hospitable solitude of our heart. Friendship is one of the most precious gifts of life, but physical proximity can be the way as well as in the way of its full realization.

A few times in my life I had the seemingly strange sensation that I felt closer to my friends in their absence than in their presence. When they were gone, I had a strong desire to meet them again but I could not avoid a certain emotion of disappointment when the meeting was realized. Our physical presence to each other prevented us from a full encounter. As if we sensed that we were more for each other than we could express. As if our individual concrete characters started functioning as a wall behind which we kept our deepest personal selves hidden. The distance created by a temporary absence helped me to see beyond their characters and revealed to me their greatness and beauty as persons which formed the basis of our love.

Kahlil Gibran wote:

> When you part from your friend, you grieve not: For that which you love most in him may be clearer in his absence, as the mountain to the climber is clearer from the plain.[10]

Living together with friends is an exceptional joy, but our lives will be sad if that becomes the aim of our strivings. Having a harmonious team working in unity of heart and mind is a gift from heaven, but if our own sense of worth depends on that situation we are sad people. Letters of friends are good to receive, but we should be able to live happily without them. Visits are gifts to be valued, but without them we should not fall into the temptation of a brooding mood. Phone calls, "just to say hello," can fill us with gratitude, but when we expect them as a necessary way to sedate our fear of being left alone, we are becoming the easy victims of our self-complaints. We are always in search of a community that can offer us a sense of belonging, but it is important to realize that being together in one place, one house, one city or one country is only secondary to the fulfillment of our legitimate desire.

Friendship and community are, first of all, inner qualities allowing human togetherness to be the playful expression of a much larger reality. They can never be claimed, planned or organized, but in our innermost self the place can be formed where they can be received as gifts.

This inner sense of friendship and community sets us free to live a "worldly" life even in the seclusion of a room, since no one should be excluded from our solitude. But it also allows us to travel light vast distances because for those who share their solitude without fear, all the ground between people has become holy ground.

So our loneliness can grow into solitude. There are days, weeks and maybe months and years during which we are so overwhelmed by our sense of loneliness that we can hardly believe that the solitude of heart is within our horizon. But when we have once sensed what this solitude can mean, we will never stop searching for it. Once we have tasted this solitude a new life becomes possible, in which we can become detached from false ties and attached to God and each other in a surprisingly new way.

Chapter 3

A CREATIVE RESPONSE

————⟫╀╀⟪————

Reactionary Life Style

The movement from loneliness to solitude is not a movement of a growing withdrawal but is instead a movement
toward a deeper engagement in the burning issues of our
time. The movement from loneliness to solitude can
make it possible to convert slowly our fearful reactions
into a loving response.

As long as we are trying to run away from our loneliness we are constantly looking for distractions with the
inexhaustible need to be entertained and kept busy. We
become the passive victims of a world asking for our
idolizing attention. We become dependent on the shift-
ing chain of events leading us into quick changes of
mood, capricious behavior and, at times, revengeful violence. Then our life becomes a spastic and often destructive sequence of actions and reactions pulling us away
from our inner selves.

It is not so difficult to see how "reactionary" we tend
to be: that is, how often our lives become a series of
nervous and often anxious reactions to the stimuli of our
surroundings. We often are very, very busy, and usually
very tired as a result, but we should ask ourselves how

much of our reading and talking, visiting and lobbying, lecturing and writing, is more part of an impulsive reaction to the changing demands of our surroundings than an action that was born out of our own center. We probably shall never reach the moment of a "pure action," and it even can be questioned how realistic or healthy it is to make that our goal. But it seems of great importance to know with an experiential knowledge the difference between an action that is triggered by a change in the surrounding scene and an action that has ripened in our hearts through careful listening to the world in which we live. The movement from loneliness to solitude should lead to a gradual conversion from an anxious reaction to a loving response. Loneliness leads to quick, often spastic, reactions which make us prisoners of our constantly changing world. But in solitude of heart we can listen to the events of the hour, the day and the year and slowly "formulate," give form to, a response that is really our own. In solitude we can pay careful attention to the world and search for an honest response.

Alertness in Solitude

Not too long ago a priest told me that he cancelled his subscription to the New York *Times* because he felt that the endless stories about war, crime, power games and political manipulation only disturbed his mind and heart and prevented him from meditation and prayer.

That is a sad story because it suggests that only by denying the world can you live in it, that only by surrounding yourself by an artificial, self-induced quietude can you live a spiritual life. A real spiritual life does exactly the opposite: it makes us so alert and aware of the world around us, that all that is and happens becomes part of our contemplation and meditation and invites us to a free and fearless response.

It is this alertness in solitude that can change our life indeed. It makes all the difference in the world how we look at and relate to our own history through which the world speaks to us.

When I look back at the last twenty years, I see that I find myself in a place and situation I had not even dreamt of when I, together with 28 classmates, prostrated myself on the floor of a Dutch Cathedral on the day of my ordination. I had hardly heard about Martin Luther King and racial problems, nor did I know the names of John F. Kennedy and Dag Hammarskjöld. I had seen the old fat Cardinal Roncalli on a pilgrimage to Padua and thought of him as an example of clerical decadency. I had read wild books about political intrigues in the Kremlin and felt happy that such things were impossible in the free world. I had heard more than I could bear about the Jewish concentration camps but realized that they belonged to a world of the older generation and were incompatible with my own. And now, only a few years later, my mind and heart are full of memories and facts that have molded me into a quite different person than I ever expected to be. Now, while able to see the end of my life cycle as well as its beginning, I realize that I have only one life to live and that it will be a life covering a period of history of which I not only am a part but which I also helped to shape. Now I see that I cannot just point to Dallas, Viet Nam, My Lai and Watergate as the explanation of why my life was different than I had foreseen, but have to search for the roots of these names in the center of my own solitude.

In our solitude, our history no longer can remain a random collection of disconnected incidents and accidents but has to become a constant call for the change of heart and mind. There we can break through the fatalistic chain of cause and effect and listen with our inner senses to the deeper meaning of the actualities of everyday life. There the world no longer is diabolic, dividing us into "fors" and "againsts" but becomes symbolic, asking us to unite and reunite the outer with the inner events. There the killing of a president, the success of a moonshot, the destruction of cities by cruel bombing and the disintegration of a government by the lust for power, as well as the many personal disappointments and pains, no longer can be seen as unavoidable concomitants of our life, but all become urgent invitations to a response; that is, a personal engagement.

Molding Interruptions

While visiting the University of Notre Dame, where I had been a teacher for a few years, I met an older experienced professor who had spent most of his life there. And while we strolled over the beautiful campus, he said with a certain melancholy in his voice, "You know, . . . my whole life I have been complaining that my work was constantly interrupted, until I discovered that my interruptions were my work."

Don't we often look at the many events of our lives as big or small interruptions, interrupting many of our plans, projects and life schemes? Don't we feel an inner protest when a student interrupts our reading, bad weather our summer, illness our well-scheduled plans, the death of a dear friend our peaceful state of mind, a cruel war our ideas about the goodness of man, and the many harsh realities of life our good dreams about it? And doesn't this unending row of interruptions build in our hearts feelings of anger, frustration and even revenge, so much so that at times we see the real possibility that growing old can become synonymous with growing bitter?

But what if our interruptions are in fact our opportunities, if they are challenges to an inner response by which growth takes place and through which we come to the fullness of being? What if the events of our history are molding us as a sculptor molds his clay, and if it is only in a careful obedience to these molding hands that we can discover our real vocation and become mature people? What if all the unexpected interruptions are in fact the invitations to give up old-fashioned and outmoded styles of living and are opening up new unexplored areas of experience? And finally: What if our history does not prove to be a blind impersonal sequence of events over which we have no control, but rather reveals to us a guiding hand pointing to a personal encounter in which all our hopes and aspirations will reach their fulfillment?

Then our life would indeed be a different life because then fate becomes opportunity, wounds a warning and paralysis an invitation to search for deeper sources of vitality. Then we can look for hope in the middle of crying cities, burning hospitals and desperate parents and children. Then we can cast off the temptation of despair and speak about the fertile tree while witnessing the dying of the seed. Then indeed we can break out of the prison of an anonymous series of events and listen to the God of history who speaks to us in the center of our solitude and respond to his ever new call for conversion.

A Contrite Heart

It is tragic to see how the religious sentiment of the
West has become so individualized that concepts such as
"a contrite heart," have come to refer only to personal
experiences of guilt and the willingness to do penance
for it. The awareness of our impurity in thoughts, words
and deeds can indeed put us in a remorseful mood and
create in us the hope for a forgiving gesture. But if the
catastrophical events of our days, the wars, mass
murders, unbridled violence, crowded prisons, torture
chambers, the hunger and illness of millions of people
and the unnamable misery of a major part of the human
race is safely kept outside the solitude of our hearts, our
contrition remains no more than a pious emotion.

The newspaper of the day on which this is written
shows a picture of three Portuguese soldiers, two of
whom are pulling out the arms of a naked prisoner while
the third cuts off his head. That same paper reports that a
Dallas policeman killed a twelve-year-old handcuffed
boy while interrogating him in a patrol car, and that a
Japanese 747 Jumbo Jet with 122 passengers was hijacked
and flown to an unknown destination. It also reveals that
the U. S. Air Force dropped 145 million dollars worth of
bombs on Cambodia during a period in which the President declared publicly that the neutrality of that country
was fully respected. It gives a gruesome description of
the electrical torture techniques used in Greece and Tur-
key. All of that "news" is simply mentioned as secondary items whereas the headlines speak about break-ins,
lies and the use of huge sums of money by the highest
officials in the government, an event described as the
greatest tragedy in the history of this country. And

today's newspaper is not different from yesterday's and is not likely to differ much from tomorrow's.

Shouldn't that crush our hearts and make us bow our heads in an endless sorrow? Shouldn't that bring all human beings who believe that life is worth living together in a common contrition and a public penance? Shouldn't that bring us finally to a confession that we as a people have sinned and need forgiveness and healing? Shouldn't this be enough to force us to break out of our individual pious shells and stretch out our arms with the words:

> From the depths I call to you, Yahweh,
> Lord, listen to my cry for help!
> Listen compassionately
>   to my pleading!
>
> If you never overlooked our sins, Yahweh,
> Lord, could anyone survive?
> But you do forgive us:
>   and for that we revere you.
>
> I wait for Yahweh, my soul waits for him,
>   I rely on his promise,
>   my soul relies on the Lord
>   more than a watchman on the coming of dawn.
>
> Let Israel rely on Yahweh
>   as much as the watchman on the dawn!
> For it is with Yahweh that mercy is to be found,
> and a generous redemption;
> it is he who redeems Israel
>   from all their sins.
> (Psalm 130)

The Burden of Reality

Can we carry the burden of reality? How can we remain open to all human tragedies and aware of the vast ocean of human suffering without becoming mentally paralyzed and depressed? How can we live a healthy and creative life when we are constantly reminded of the fate of the millions who are poor, sick, hungry and persecuted? How can we even smile when we keep being confronted by pictures of tortures and executions?

I do not know the answer to these questions. There are people in our midst who have allowed the pain of the world to enter so deeply into their hearts that it has become their vocation to remind us constantly, mostly against our will, of the sins of this world. There are even a few saints who have become so much a part of the human condition and have identified themselves to such a degree with the misery of their fellow human beings that they refuse happiness for themselves as long as there are suffering people in this world. Although they irritate us and although we would like to dispose of them by labeling them masochists or doomsday prophets, they are indispensable reminders that no lasting healing will ever take place without a solidarity of heart. These few "extremists" or "fanatics" force us to ask ourselves how many games we play with ourselves and how many walls we keep erecting to prevent ourselves from knowing and feeling the burden of human solidarity.

Maybe, for the time being, we have to accept the many fluctuations between knowing and not knowing, seeing and not seeing, feeling and not feeling, between days in which the whole world seems like a rose garden and days in which our hearts seem tied to a millstone, between moments of ecstatic joy and moments of gloomy depression, between the humble confession that the newspaper holds more than our souls can bear and the realization that it is only through facing up to the reality of our world that we can grow into our own responsibility. Maybe we have to be tolerant toward our own avoidances and denials in the conviction that we cannot force ourselves to face what we are not ready to respond to and in the hope that in one future day we will have the courage and strength to open our eyes fully and see without being destroyed. All this might be the case as long as we remember that there is no hope in denial or avoidance, neither for ourselves nor for anyone else, and that new life can only be born out of the seed planted in crushed soil. Indeed God, our Lord, "will not scorn this crushed and broken heart" (Psalm 51:17).

What keeps us from opening ourselves to the reality of the world? Could it be that we cannot accept our power-lessness and are only willing to see those wounds that we can heal? Could it be that we do not want to give up our illusion that we are masters over our world and, there-fore, create our own Disneyland where we can make ourselves believe that all events of life are safely under control? Could it be that our blindness and deafness are signs of our own resistance to acknowledging that we are not the Lord of the Universe? It is hard to allow these questions to go beyond the level of rhetoric and to really sense in our innermost self how much we resent our powerlessness.

Protest Out of Solitude

But life can teach us that although the events of the day are out of our hands, they should never be out of our hearts, that instead of becoming bitter our lives can yield to the wisdom that only from the heart a creative re-sponse can come forth. When the answer to our world remains hanging between our minds and our hands, it remains weak and superficial. When our protests against war, segregation and social injustice do not reach beyond the level of a reaction, then our indignation becomes self-righteous, our hope for a better world degenerates into a desire for quick results, and our generosity is soon exhausted by disappointments. Only when our mind has descended into our heart can we expect a lasting response to well up from our innermost self.

Many of those who worked hard for civil rights and were very active in the peace movement of the sixties have grown tired and often cynical. When they discovered that the situation was out of their hands, that little could be done, that no visible changes took place, they lost their vitality and fell back on their wounded selves, escaped into a world of dreams and fantasies, or joined spitefully the crowd they had been protesting against. It is, therefore, not surprising to find many of the old activists struggling with their frustrations in psychotherapy, denying them by drugs or trying to alleviate them in the context of new cults. If any criticism can be made of the sixties, it is not that protest was meaningless but that it was not deep enough, in the sense that it was not rooted in the solitude of the heart. When only our minds and hands work together we quickly become dependent on the results of our actions and tend to give up when they do not materialize. In the solitude of the heart we can truly listen to the pains of the world because there we can recognize them not as strange and unfamiliar pains, but as pains that are indeed our own. There we can see that what is most universal is most personal and that indeed nothing human is strange to us. There we can feel that the cruel reality of history is indeed the reality of the human heart, our own included, and that to protest asks, first of all, for a confession of our own participation in the human condition. There we can indeed respond.

It would be paralyzing to proclaim that we, as individuals, are responsible for all human suffering, but it is a liberating message to say that we are called to respond to it. Because out of an inner solidarity with our fellow humans the first attempts to alleviate these pains can come forth.

Compassion

It is this inner solidarity which prevents self-righteousness and makes compassion possible. Thomas Merton, the monk, expresses this well when he writes:

> Once God has called you to solitude, everything you touch leads you further into solitude. Everything that affects you builds you into a hermit, as long as you do not insist on doing the work yourself and building your own kind of hermitage. What is my new desert? The name of it is compassion. There is no wilderness so terrible, so beautiful, so arid and so fruitful as the wilderness of compassion. It is the only desert that shall truly flourish like the lily. It shall become a pool, it shall bud forth and blossom and rejoice with joy. It is in the desert of compassion that the thirsty land turns into springs of water, that the poor possess all things.[1]

The paradox of Merton's life indeed is that his withdrawal from the world brought him into closer contact with it. The more he was able to convert his restless loneliness into a solitude of heart, the more he could discover the pains of his world in his own inner center and respond to them. His compassionate solidarity with the human struggle made him a spokesman for many who, although lacking his talent for writing, shared his solitude. How much Merton became aware of his responsibilities in solitude becomes clear when he writes:

That I should have been born in 1915, that I should be the contemporary of Auschwitz, Hiroshima, Viet Nam and the Watts riots are things about which I was not first consulted. Yet they are also events in which, whether I like it or not, I am deeply and personally involved.[2]

And not without a touch of sarcasm he adds:

. . . it has become transparently obvious that mere automatic "rejection of the world" and "contempt for the world" is in fact not a choice but the evasion of a choice. The man who pretends that he can turn his back on Auschwitz, or Viet Nam and act as if they were not there is simply bluffing. I think that this is getting to be generally admitted, even by monks.[3]

Compassion born in solitude makes us very much aware of our own historicity. We are not called to respond to generalities but to the concrete facts with which we are confronted day after day. A compassionate man can no longer look at these manifestations of evil and death as disturbing interruptions of his life plan but rather has to confront them as an opportunity for the conversion of himself and his fellow human beings. Every time in history that men and women have been able to respond to the events of their world as an occasion to change their hearts, an inexhaustible source of generosity and new life has been opened, offering hope far beyond the limits of human prediction.

Solidarity in Pain

When we think about the people who have given us hope and have increased the strength of our soul, we might discover that they were not the advice givers,

warners or moralists, but the few who were able to articulate in words and actions the human condition in which
we participate and who encouraged us to face the realities of life. Preachers who reduce mysteries to problems
and offer Band-Aid-type solutions are depressing because they avoid the compassionate solidarity out of
which healing comes forth. But Tolstoy's description of
the complex emotions of Anna Karenina, driving her to
suicide, and Graham Greene's presentation of the burned
out case of the Belgian architect Querry, whose search
for meaning leads him to his death in the African jungle,
can give us a new sense of hope. Not because of any
solution they offered but because of the courage to enter
so deeply into human suffering and speak from there.
Neither Kierkegaard nor Sartre nor Camus nor Hammarskjöld nor Solzhenitsyn has offered solutions, but
many who read their words find new strength to pursue
their own personal search. Those who do not run away
from our pains but touch them with compassion bring
healing and new strength. The paradox indeed is that the
beginning of healing is in the solidarity with the pain. In
our solution-oriented society it is more important than
ever to realize that wanting to alleviate pain without
sharing it is like wanting to save a child from a burning
house without the risk of being hurt. It is in solitude that
this compassionate solidarity takes its shape.

The movement from loneliness to solitude, therefore,
is not a movement of a growing withdrawal from, but
rather a movement toward, a deeper engagement in the
burning issues of our time. The movement from loneliness to solitude is a movement that allows us to perceive
interruptions as occasions for a conversion of heart,
which makes our responsibilities a vocation instead of a
burden, and which creates the inner space where a compassionate solidarity with our fellow human beings be-

comes possible. The movement from loneliness to solitude is a movement by which we reach out to our innermost being to find there our great healing powers, not as a unique property to be defended but as a gift to be shared with all human beings. And so, the movement from loneliness to solitude leads us spontaneously to the movement from hostility to hospitality. It is this second movement that can encourage us to reach out creatively to the many whom we meet on our way.

REACHING OUT TO OUR
FELLOW HUMAN BEINGS

---•+•---

The Second Movement:
From Hostility to Hospitality

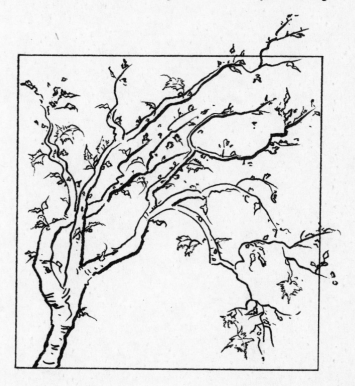

Chapter 4

CREATING SPACE FOR STRANGERS

———————————⟩╂ ╂⟨———————————

Living in a World of Strangers

The first characteristic of the spiritual life is the continuing movement from loneliness to solitude. Its second equally important characteristic is the movement by which our hostilities can be converted into hospitality. It is there that our changing relationship to ourself can be brought to fruition in an ever-changing relationship to our fellow human beings. It is there that our reaching out to our innermost being can lead to a reaching out to the many strangers whom we meet on our way through life. In our world full of strangers, estranged from their own past, culture and country, from their neighbors, friends and family, from their deepest self and their God, we witness a painful search for a hospitable place where life can be lived without fear and where community can be found. Although many, we might even say most, strangers in this world become easily the victim of a fearful hostility, it is possible for men and women and obligatory for Christians to offer an open and hospitable space where strangers can cast off their strangeness and become our fellow human beings. The movement from hostility to hospitality is hard and full of difficulties. Our society seems to be increasingly full of fearful, defensive, aggressive people anxiously clinging to their property and inclined to look at their surrounding world with suspicion, always expecting an enemy to suddenly appear, intrude and do harm. But still—that is our vocation: to convert the *hostis* into a *hospes*, the enemy into a guest and to create the free and fearless space where brotherhood and sisterhood can be formed and fully experienced.

A Biblical Term

At first the word "hospitality" might evoke the image of soft sweet kindness, tea parties, bland conversations and a general atmosphere of coziness. Probably this has its good reasons since in our culture the concept of hospitality has lost much of its power and is often used in circles where we are more prone to expect a watered down piety than a serious search for an authentic Christian spirituality. But still, if there is any concept worth restoring to its original depth and evocative potential, it is the concept of hospitality. It is one of the richest biblical terms that can deepen and broaden our insight in our relationships to our fellow human beings. Old and New Testament stories not only show how serious our obligation is to welcome the stranger in our home, but they also tell us that guests are carrying precious gifts with them, which they are eager to reveal to a receptive host. When Abraham received three strangers at Mamre and offered them water, bread and a fine tender calf, they revealed themselves to him as the Lord announcing that Sarah his wife would give birth to a son (Genesis 18:1–15). When the widow of Zarephath offered food and shelter to Elijah, he revealed himself as a man of God offering her an abundance of oil and meal and raising her son from the dead (I Kings 17:9–24). When the two trav-

elers to Emmaus invited the stranger, who had joined
them on the road to stay with them for the night, he
made himself known in the breaking of the bread as
their Lord and Saviour (Luke 24:13–35).

When hostility is converted into hospitality then fearful strangers can become guests revealing to their hosts
the promise they are carrying with them. Then, in fact,
the distinction between host and guest proves to be artificial and evaporates in the recognition of the new found
unity.

Thus the biblical stories help us to realize not just that
hospitality is an important virtue, but even more that in
the context of hospitality guest and host can reveal their
most precious gifts and bring new life to each other.

During the last decades psychology has made great
contributions to a new understanding of interpersonal
relationships. Not only psychiatrists and clinical psychologists, but also social workers, occupational ther-
apists, ministers, priests and many others working in the
helping professions have made grateful use of these new
insights in their work. But maybe some of us have become so impressed by these new findings that we have
lost sight of the great wealth contained and preserved in
such ancient concepts as hospitality. Maybe the concept
of hospitality can offer a new dimension to our understanding of a healing relationship and the formation of a
re-creative community in a world so visibly suffering
from alienation and estrangement.

The term hospitality, therefore, should not be limited
to its literal sense of receiving a stranger in our house—
although it is important never to forget or neglect that!—
but as a fundamental attitude toward our fellow human
being, which can be expressed in a great variety of ways.

Ambivalence Toward the Stranger

Although it belongs to the core of a Christian spirituality to reach out to strangers and invite them into our lives, it is important to realize clearly that our spontaneous feelings toward strangers are quite ambivalent. It does not require much social analysis to recognize how many forms of hostility, usually pervaded with fear and anxiety, prevent us from inviting people into our world.

To fully appreciate what hospitality can mean, we possibly have to become first a stranger ourselves. A student wrote:

> I left Nice one day with little money and stuck out my thumb. For five days I went wherever the wind blew me. I ran out of money and had to depend on the kindness of others. I learned what it is to be humble, thankful for a meal, a ride, and totally at the mercy of chance . . .

We can say that during the last years strangers have become more and more subject to hostility than to hospitality. In fact, we have protected our apartments with dogs and double locks, our buildings with vigilant doormen, our roads with anti-hitchhike signs, our subways with security guards, our airports with safety officials, our cities with armed police and our country with an omnipresent military. Although we might want to show sympathy for the poor, the lonely, the homeless and the rejected, our feelings toward a stranger knocking on our door and asking for food and shelter is ambivalent at the least. In general we do not expect much from strangers. We say to each other: "You better hide your money, lock your door and chain your bike." People who are unfamiliar, speak another language, have another color, wear a different type of clothes and live a life style different from ours, make us afraid and even hostile. Frequently we return home from vacation with that gnawing suspicion that some stranger might have broken into our home and discovered the closet where we have hidden our "valuables."

In our world the assumption is that strangers are a potential danger and that it is up to them to disprove it. When we travel we keep a careful eye on our luggage; when we walk the streets we are aware of where we keep our money; and when we walk at night in a dark park our whole body is tense with fear of an attack. Our heart might desire to help others: to feed the hungry, visit the prisoners and offer a shelter to travelers; but meanwhile we have surrounded ourselves with a wall of fear and hostile feelings, instinctively avoiding people and places where we might be reminded of our good intentions.

It really does not have to be so dramatic. Fear and hostility are not limited to our encounters with burglars, drug addicts or strangely behaving types. In a world so pervaded with competition, even those who are very close to each other, such as classmates, teammates, co-actors in a play, colleagues in work, can become infected by fear and hostility when they experience each other as a threat to their intellectual or professional safety. Many places that are created to bring people closer together and help them form a peaceful community have degenerated into mental battlefields. Students in classrooms, teachers in faculty meetings, staff members in hospitals and co-workers in projects often find themselves paralyzed by mutual hostility, unable to realize their purposes because of fear, suspicion, and even blatant aggression. Sometimes institutions explicitly created to offer free time and free space to develop the most precious human potentials have become so dominated by hostile defensiveness that some of the best ideas and some of the most valuable feelings remain unexpressed. Grades, exams, selective systems, promotion chances and desires for awards often block the manifestation of the best that man can produce.

The Recognition of Back-stage Hostility

Recently an actor told me stories about his professional world which seemed symbolic of much of our contemporary situation. While rehearsing the most moving scenes of love, tenderness and intimate relationships, the actors were so jealous of each other and so full of apprehension about their chances to "make it," that the back-stage scene was one of hatred, harshness and mutual suspicion. Those who kissed each other on the stage were tempted to hit each other behind it, and those who portrayed the most profound human emotions of love in the footlights displayed the most trivial and hostile rivalries as soon as the footlights had dimmed.

Much of our world is similar to the acting stage on which peace, justice and love are portrayed by actors who cripple each other by mutual hostilities. Aren't there many doctors, priests, lawyers, social workers, psychologists and counselors who started their studies and work with a great desire to be of service but find themselves soon victimized by the intense rivalries and hostilities in their own personal as well as professional circles? Many ministers and priests who announce peace and love from the pulpit cannot find much of it in their own rectory around their own table. Many social workers trying to heal family conflicts struggle with the same at home. And how many of us don't feel an inner apprehension when we hear our own pains in the story of those who ask our help?

But maybe it is exactly this paradox that can give us our healing power. When we have seen and acknowledged our own hostilities and fears without hesitation, it is more likely that we also will be able to sense from within the other pole toward which we want to lead not only ourselves but our neighbors as well. The act on the stage of our life will probably always look better than what goes on behind the curtains, but as long as we are willing to face the contrast and struggle to minimize it the tension can keep us humble by allowing us to offer our service to others, without being whole ourselves.

Creating a Free and Friendly Space

When we have become sensitive to the painful contours of our hostility we can start identifying the lines of its opposite toward which we are called to move: hospitality. The German word of hospitality is *Gastfreundschaft* which means, friendship for the guest. The Dutch use the word *gastvrijheid* which means, the freedom of the guest. Although this might reflect that the Dutch people find freedom more important than friendship, it definitively shows that hospitality wants to offer friendship without binding the guest and freedom without leaving him alone.

Hospitality, therefore, means primarily the creation of a free space where the stranger can enter and become a friend instead of an enemy. Hospitality is not to change people, but to offer them space where change can take place. It is not to bring men and women over to our side, but to offer freedom not disturbed by dividing lines. It is not to lead our neighbor into a corner where there are no alternatives left, but to open a wide spectrum of options

for choice and commitment. It is not an educated intimi-
dation with good books, good stories and good works,
but the liberation of fearful hearts so that words can find
roots and bear ample fruit. It is not a method of making
our God and our way into the criteria of happiness, but
the opening of an opportunity to others to find their God
and their way. The paradox of hospitality is that it wants
to create emptiness, not a fearful emptiness, but a
friendly emptiness where strangers can enter and discover themselves as created free; free to sing their own
songs, speak their own languages, dance their own
dances; free also to leave and follow their own vocations.
Hospitality is not a subtle invitation to adopt the life
style of the host, but the gift of a chance for the guest to
find his own.

Thoreau gives a good example of this attitude when he
writes:

> I would not have anyone adopt *my* mode of living on
> any account; for, beside that before he has fairly
> learned it I may have found out another for myself, I
> desire that there may be as many different persons in
> the world as possible; but I would have each one be
> very careful to find out and pursue *his own* way, and
> not his father's or his mother's or his neighbor's in-
> stead.[1]

Creating space for the other is far from an easy task. It
requires hard concentration and articulate work. It is like
the task of a patrolman trying to create some space in the
middle of a mob of panic-driven people for an ambu-
lance to reach the center of the accident. Indeed, more
often than not rivalry and competition, desire for power
and immediate results, impatience and frustration, and,
most of all, plain fear make their forceful demands and
tend to fill every possible empty corner of our life.

Empty space tends to create fear. As long as our minds hearts and hands are occupied we can avoid confronting the painful questions, to which we never gave much attention and which we do not want to surface. "Being busy" has become a status symbol, and most people keep encouraging each other to keep their body and mind in constant motion. From a distance, it appears that we try to keep each other filled with words and actions, without tolerance for a moment of silence. Hosts often feel that they have to talk all the time to their guests and entertain them with things to do, places to see and people to visit. But by filling up every empty corner and occupying every empty time their hospitality becomes more oppressing than revealing.

Occupied and Preoccupied Space

Occupation and not empty space is what most of us are looking for. When we are not occupied we become restless. We even become fearful when we do not know what we will do the next hour, the next day or the next year. Then occupation is called a blessing and emptiness a curse. Many telephone conversations start with the words: "I know you are busy, but . . ." and we would confuse the speaker and even harm our reputation were we to say, "Oh no, I am completely free, today, tomorrow and the whole week." Our client might well lose interest in a man who has so little to do.

Being busy, active and on the move has nearly become part of our constitution. When we are asked to sit in a chair, without a paper to read, a radio to listen to, a television to watch, without a visitor or a phone, we are inclined to become so restless and tense that we welcome anything that will distract us again.

This explains why silence is such a difficult task. Many people who say how much they desire silence, rest, quietude would find it nearly impossible to bear the stillness of a monastery. When all the movements around them have stopped, when nobody asks them a question, seeks advice or even offers a helping hand, when there is no music or newspapers they quite often experience such an inner restlessness that they will grab any opportunity to become involved again. The first weeks or even months in a contemplative monastery, therefore, are not always as restful as they might seem, and it is indeed not surprising that vacations are more often spent on busy beaches, camping grounds and around entertainment centers than in the silence of monasteries.

All this shows that preoccupation is in fact a greater stumbling block than occupation. We are so afraid of open spaces and empty places that we occupy them with our minds even before we are there. Our worries and concerns are expressions of our inability to leave unresolved questions unresolved and open-ended situations open-ended. They make us grab any possible solution and answer that seems to fit the occasion. They reveal our intolerance of the incomprehensibility of people and events and make us look for labels or classifications to fill the emptiness with self-created illusions.

We indeed have become very preoccupied people, afraid of unnamable emptiness and silent solitude. In fact, our preoccupations prevent our having new experiences and keep us hanging on to the familiar ways. Preoccupations are our fearful ways of keeping things the same, and it often seems that we prefer a bad certainty to a good uncertainty. Our preoccupations help us to maintain the personal world we have created over the years and block the way to revolutionary change. Our fears,

uncertainties and hostilities make us fill our inner world
with ideas, opinions, judgments and values to which we
cling as to a precious property. Instead of facing the challenge of new worlds opening themselves for us, and
struggling in the open field, we hide behind the walls of
our concerns holding on to the familiar life items we
have collected in the past.

The conservative power of our preoccupation is very
convincingly expressed by Don Juan, the Yaqui Indian, in
one of his conversations with the anthropologist Carlos
Castaneda. One day Carlos asked Don Juan how he
could better live in accordance with the Indian's teaching. "You think and talk too much, you must stop talking
to yourself," Don Juan answered. He explained that we
maintain our world by our inner talk, and that we talk to
ourselves until everything is as it should be, repeating
our inner choices over and over, staying always on the
same paths. If we would stop telling ourselves that the
world is such and so, it would cease to be so! Don Juan
didn't think that Carlos was ready for such a blow, but
he advised his student to listen to the world and so allow
changes to take place.[2]

Although this advice might sound bizarre to the ears
of the "organization man," it should not be strange for
someone who has taken to heart the words of Jesus
Christ. Didn't he also say that our worries prevent us
from letting the kingdom, that is, the new world, come?
Don Juan is asking how we ever can expect something
really new to happen to us if our hearts and minds are so
full of our own concerns that we do not even listen to
the sounds announcing a new reality. And Jesus says:
". . . do not worry; do not say, 'What are we to eat?
What are we to drink? How are we to be clothed?' It is
the pagans who set their hearts on all these things. Your

heavenly Father knows you need them all. Set your hearts on his kingdom first, and on his righteousness, and all these other things will be given you as well. So do not worry about tomorrow: tomorrow will take care of itself" (Matthew 6:31–34).

So we can see that creating space is far from easy in our occupied and preoccupied society. And still, if we expect any salvation, redemption, healing and new life, the first thing we need is an open receptive place where something can happen to us. Hospitality, therefore, is such an important attitude. We cannot change the world by a new plan, project or idea. We cannot even change other people by our convictions, stories, advice and proposals, but we can offer a space where people are encouraged to disarm themselves, to lay aside their occupations and preoccupations and to listen with attention and care to the voices speaking in their own center. How important it is to become empty in order that we may learn is well illustrated in the following Zen story:

> Nan-in, a Japanese master during the Meiji era (1868–1912) received a university professor who came to inquire about Zen. Nan-in served tea. He poured his visitor's cup full, and then kept pouring. The professor watched the overflow until he could no longer restrain himself. "It is overfull. No more will go in!" "Like this cup," Nan-in said, "you are full of your opinions and speculations. How can I show you Zen unless you first empty your cup?"[3]

To convert hostility into hospitality requires the creation of the friendly empty space where we can reach out to our fellow human beings and invite them to a new relationship. This conversion is an inner event that cannot be manipulated but must develop from within. Just as we cannot force a plant to grow but can take away the weeds and stones which prevent its development, so we cannot force anyone to such a personal and intimate change of heart, but we can offer the space where such a change can take place.

Chapter 5

FORMS OF HOSPITALITY

The "Ins" and "Outs" of Our Relationships

The movement from hostility to hospitality is a movement that determines our relationship to other people. We probably will never be free from all our hostilities, and there even may be days and weeks in which our hostile feelings dominate our emotional life to such a degree that the best thing we can do is to keep distance, speak little to others and not write letters, except to ourselves. Sometimes events in our lives breed feelings of bitterness, jealousy, suspicion and even desires for revenge, which need time to be healed. It is realistic to realize that although we hope to move toward hospitality, life is too complex to expect a one-way direction. But when we make ourselves aware of the hospitality we have enjoyed from others and are grateful for the few moments in which we can create some space ourselves, we may become more sensitive to our inner movements and be more able to affirm an open attitude toward our fellow human beings.

Looking at hospitality as the creation of a free and friendly space where we can reach out to strangers and invite them to become our friends, it is clear that this can take place on many levels and in many relationships. Although the word stranger suggests someone who belongs to another world than ours, speaks another language and has different customs, it is important, first of all, to recognize the stranger in our own familiar circle. When we are able to be good hosts for the strangers in our midst we may find also ways to expand our hospitality to broader horizons. Therefore, it might be worthwhile to look carefully at three types of relationships that can be better understood from the perspective of hospitality: the relationship between parents and their children, the relationship between teachers and their students, and the relationship between professionals—such as doctors, social workers, psychologists, counselors, nurses, ministers and priests—and their patients, clients, counselees and parishioners.

In all three types of relationships we become involved at some point in our own history. The complexity of life is exactly related to the fact that often we find ourselves involved in all three types of relationships at the same time and on both sides. While being a father to our children, a teacher to our students and a counselor to our counselees, we also remain child, student and patient in other contexts. While trying to be a good mother, we often still have responsibilities as daughter; while teaching in the daytime, we might be sitting on the other side of the classroom in the evening; and while giving advice to others, we realize at times how badly we need it ourselves. We all are children and parents, students and teachers, healers and in need of care. And so we move in and out of each others' worlds at different times in different ways. While the complexity of these many "ins" and "outs" have created a still-growing number of studies, research projects, books and institutes, the concept of hospitality might bring a unifying dimension to all these interpersonal relationships. It might help us see how they all stand together under the great commandment: "You must love your neighbour as yourself" (Mark 12:31).

Parents and Children

It may sound strange to speak of the relationship between parents and children in terms of hospitality. But it belongs to the center of the Christian message that children are not properties to own and rule over, but gifts to cherish and care for. Our children are our most important guests, who enter into our home, ask for careful attention, stay for a while and then leave to follow their own way. Children are strangers whom we have to get to know. They have their own style, their own rhythm and their own capacities for good and evil. They cannot be explained by looking at their parents. It is, therefore, not surprising to hear parents say about their children, "They are all different, none is like the other and they keep surprising and amazing us." Fathers and mothers, more than their family and friends, are often aware how their children differ from themselves and each other. Children carry a promise with them, a hidden treasure that has to be led into the open through education (e = out; *ducere* = to lead) in a hospitable home. It takes much time and patience to make the little stranger feel at home, and it is realistic to say that parents have to learn to love their children. Sometimes a father or mother will be honest and free enough to say that he or she looked at the new baby as at a stranger without feeling any special affection, not because the child was unwanted but because love is not an automatic reaction. It comes forth out of a relationship which has to grow and deepen. We can even say that the love between parents and children develops and matures to the degree that they can reach out to each other and discover each other as fellow human beings, who have much to share and whose differences in age, talents and behavior are much less important than their common humanity.

What parents can offer is a home, a place that is receptive but also has the safe boundaries within which their children can develop and discover what is helpful and what is harmful. There their children can ask questions without fear and can experiment with life without taking the risk of rejection. There they can be encouraged to listen to their own inner selves and to develop the freedom that gives them the courage to leave the home and travel on. The hospitable home indeed is the place where father, mother and children can reveal their talents to each other, become present to each other as members of the same human family and support each other in their common struggles to live and make live.

The awareness that children are guests can be a liberating awareness because many parents suffer from deep guilt feelings toward their children, thinking that they are responsible for everything their sons or daughters do. When they see their child living in ways they disapprove of, the parents may castigate themselves with the questions: "What did we do wrong? What should we have done to prevent this behavior?" and they may wonder where they failed. But children are not properties we can control as a puppeteer controls his puppets, or train as a lion tamer trains his lions. They are guests we have to respond to, not possessions we are responsible for.

Many parents question the value of baptism of newborn babies. But one important aspect of early baptism is that when the parents bring their child to the church, they are reminded that the child is not their own private property but a gift of God given to a community that is

much larger than the immediate family. In our culture it
seems that all the responsibility for the child rests on the
biological parents. The high-rise apartment buildings, in
which families live in their small isolated units and are
often fearful of their neighbors, do indeed not offer the
small child much more to depend on than his own parents.

> During a visit in Mexico, sitting on a bench in one of
> the village plazas, I saw how much larger the family of
> the children was. They were hugged, kissed and car-
> ried around by aunts, uncles, friends and neighbors,
> and it seemed that the whole community spending its
> evening playfully in the plaza became father and
> mother for the little ones. Their affection, and their
> fearless movements made me aware that for them ev-
> eryone was family.

The church is perhaps one of the few places left where
we can meet people who are different than we are but
with whom we can form a larger family. Taking our children out of the house and bringing them to the church
for baptism is at least an important reminder of the larger
community in which they are born and which can offer
them a free space to grow to maturity without fear.

The difficult task of parenthood is to help children
grow to the freedom that permits them to stand on their
own feet, physically, mentally and spiritually and to allow them to move away in their own direction. The
temptation is, and always remains, to cling to our children, to use them for our own unfulfilled needs and to
hold on to them, suggesting in many direct and indirect
ways that they owe us so much. It indeed is hard to see
our children leave after many years of much love and
much work to bring them to maturity, but when we keep
reminding ourselves that they are just guests who have

their own destination, which we do not know or dictate, we might be more able to let them go in peace and with our blessing. A good host is not only able to receive his guests with honor and offer them all the care they need but also to let them go when their time to leave has come.

Teachers and Students

Not only in the relationships between parents and their children but also in those between teachers and their students, hospitality can be seen as a model for a creative interchange between people. If there is any area that needs a new spirit, a redemptive and liberating spirituality, it is the area of education in which so many people spend their lives, or at least crucial parts of their lives, as students or teachers or both. One of the greatest tragedies of our culture is that millions of young people spend many hours, days, weeks and years listening to lectures, reading books and writing papers with a constantly increasing resistance. This has become such a widespread phenomenon that teachers on all levels, from grade school to graduate school, are complimented and praised when they can get the attention of their students and motivate them to do their work. Practically every student perceives his education as a long endless row of obligations to be fulfilled. If there is any culture that has succeeded in killing the natural spontaneous curiosity of people and dulling the human desire to know, it is our technocratic society.

As teachers, we have even become insensitive to the ridiculous situation in which adult men and women feel that they "owe" us a paper of at least twenty pages. We have lost our sense of surprise when men and women who are taking courses about the questions of life and death anxiously ask us how much is "required." Instead of spending a number of free years searching for the value and meaning of our human existence with the help of others who expressed their own experiences in word or writing, most students are constantly trying to "earn" credits, degrees and awards, willing to sacrifice even their own growth.

In such a climate is it not surprising that an enormous resistance to learning develops and that much real mental and emotional development is inhibited by an educational situation in which students perceive their teachers more as demanding bosses than as guides in their search for knowledge and understanding.

One of the greatest problems of education remains that solutions are offered without the existence of a question. It seems that the least-used source of formation and information is the experience of the students themselves. Sometimes teachers speak about love and hate, fear and joy, hope and despair while students make obedient notes or look out the window in boredom. This is understandable only when we realize that the students themselves have not had the opportunity to make their own experience of love and hate, fear and joy, hope and despair available to themselves and allow their real questions to be born from their personal source. But in a hostile climate nobody wants to become vulnerable and make it known to himself, his fellow students or his teacher that some of the most central questions of life are still untouched.

Teaching, therefore, asks first of all the creation of a space where students and teachers can enter into a fearless communication with each other and allow their respective life experiences to be their primary and most valuable source of growth and maturation. It asks for a mutual trust in which those who teach and those who want to learn can become present to each other, not as opponents, but as those who share in the same struggle and search for the same truth.

I remember a student presenting with great enthusiasm a summary of a book on Zen meditation while his own life experiences of restlessness, loneliness and desire for solitude and quietude remained an unknown book of knowledge to him. Just as words can become obstacles for communication, books can prevent self-knowledge.

Teaching situations in which students as well as teachers are deeply affected by fear of rejection, by doubt and insecurity about their own abilities, and by an often-unexpressed anger toward each other are countereducational. Nobody will show his most precious talent to those whom he fears.

But is it possible to become hospitable to each other in a classroom? It is far from easy since both teachers and students are part of a very demanding, pushing and often exploitative society in which personal growth and development have become secondary to the ability to produce and earn not only credits but a living. In such a production-oriented society even schools no longer have the time or space where the questions about why we live and love, work and die can be raised without fear of competition, rivalry or concerns about punishment or rewards.

And still teaching, from the point of view of a Christian spirituality, means the commitment to provide the fearless space where such questions can come to consciousness and can be responded to, not by prefabricated answers, but by an articulate encouragement to enter them seriously and personally. When we look at teaching in terms of hospitality, we can say that the teacher is called upon to create for his students a free and fearless space where mental and emotional development can take place. When we want to speak about the "spirituality of the teacher," two aspects of his task ask for special attention: revealing and affirming.

The hospitable teacher has to reveal to the students that they have something to offer. Many students have been for so many years on the receiving side and have become so deeply impregnated with the idea that there is still a lot more to learn, that they have lost confidence in themselves and can hardly imagine that they themselves have something to give, not only to the ones who are less educated but to their fellow students and teachers as well.

Therefore, the teacher has first of all to reveal, to take away the veil covering many students' intellectual life, and help them see that their own life experiences, their own insights and convictions, their own intuitions and formulations are worth serious attention. A good host is the one who believes that his guest is carrying a promise he wants to reveal to anyone who shows genuine interest. It is so easy to impress students with books they have not read, with terms they have not heard, or with situations with which they are unfamiliar. It is much more difficult to be a receiver who can help the students to distinguish carefully between the wheat and the weeds in their own lives and to show the beauty of the gifts they are carrying with them. We will never believe that we have anything to give unless there is someone who is able to receive. Indeed, we discover our gifts in the eyes of the receiver. Teachers who can detach themselves from their need to impress and control, and who can allow themselves to become receptive for the news that their students carry with them, will find that it is in receptivity that gifts become visible.

What is revealed as good, worthwhile or as a new contribution, needs to be affirmed. Affirmation, encouragement and support are often much more important than criticism. The good host is the one who not only helps the guests to see that they have hidden talents, but who also is able to help them develop and deepen these talents so that they can continue their way on their own with a renewed self-confidence. Self-doubt is such a rampant disease in many schools that affirmation is more important than ever. Affirmation can mean many things. It can simply mean the expression of excitement and surprise or a word of thanks. It can mean recommendations of good books or referral to people with special talents. It often means just bringing the right persons together or setting apart time and place where more thinking can be done. But it always includes the inner conviction that a precious gift merits attention and continuing care.

Especially in religious education, revelation and affirmation are of great importance. The fact that so many students do not care for religious instruction is largely related to the fact that their own life experience is hardly touched. There are just as many ways to be a Christian as there are Christians, and it seems that more important than the imposition of any doctrine or precoded idea is to offer the students the place where they can reveal their great human potentials to love, to give, and to create, and where they can find the affirmation that gives them the courage to continue their search without fear.

Only when we have come in touch with our own life experiences and have learned to listen to our inner cravings for liberation and new life can we realize that Jesus did not just speak, but that he reached out to us in our most personal needs. The Gospel doesn't just contain ideas worth remembering. It is a message responding to our individual human condition. The Church is not an institution forcing us to follow its rules. It is a commu-

nity of people inviting us to still our hunger and thirst at
its tables. Doctrines are not alien formulations which we
must adhere to but the documentation of the most profound human experiences which, transcending time and
place, are handed over from generation to generation as a
light in our darkness.

But what is the sense of speaking about light to people
who do not sense their darkness? Why should we speak
about the Way to someone who does not realize that
there are many roads? How can anyone desire the truth
when he or she doesn't even know that there are questions? It is not surprising that many find religious education boring, superfluous, and unnecessary, and that they
complain that it creates fear instead of joy, mental im-
prisonment instead of spiritual freedom. But those who
have been able to find a place of rest and inner solitude
and have listened carefully to the questions arising from
their own hearts will also recognize that words spoken in
such a place are words not to hurt but to heal.

Thus, revelation and affirmation are two important aspects of the relationship between teachers and their students. Both aspects show that students are not just the
poor, needy, ignorant beggars who come to the man or
woman of knowledge, but that they are indeed like
guests who honor the house with their visit and will not
leave it without having made their own contribution. To
look at teaching as a form of hospitality might free it
from some of its unreal heaviness and bring some of its
exhilarating moments back into perspective.

Just as parents are tempted to relate to their children as
properties, so also teachers can develop a similar attitude
toward their students. In fact, many teachers often become sad and depressed because of their possessive sense
of responsibility. They feel unhappy or even guilty when

students do not accept their ideas, advice or suggestions, and often they suffer from a deep sense of inadequacy.

When we are teachers it is good, therefore, to realize that students cannot be molded into one special form of the good life, but are only temporary visitors who have been in many rooms before they came into ours. Our relationship with our students is first of all a relationship in which we offer ourselves to our searching students, to help them develop some clarity in the many impressions of their mind and heart and discover patterns of thoughts and feelings on which they can build their own life. By a supportive presence we can offer the space with safe boundaries within which our students can give up their defensive stance and bend over their own life experience, with all its strong and weak sides, to find the beginnings of a plan worth following. As teachers we have to encourage our students to reflection which leads to vision—theirs, not ours.

It is, however, only realistic to say that many students have become so tired of the demands of the educational institutions they have to go through and so suspicious of anyone who expects something new, that they can seldom respond to a really hospitable teacher and take the risk of trust—trust in him and in themselves. On the other hand, it is also true that many highly motivated teachers have become so tired of trying to "reach" their students, and so exhausted by the demands put on them by the great, often anonymous, structures within which they have to work, that their hospitality quickly degenerates into defensiveness. Instead of revealing and affirming, they have found themselves demanding and policing, sometimes even exploding and taking revenge. It is, therefore, not so surprising that many schools are often more effective in producing bitter rivals than in forming receptive hosts.

Healers and Patients

Finally, all those who want to reach out to their fellow human beings in the context of one of the many helping professions, as doctors, social workers, counselors, ministers or in many other capacities, have to keep reminding themselves that they do not own anyone who is in need of care. The great danger of the increasing professionalization of the different forms of healing is that they become ways of exercising power instead of offering service. It is easy to observe that many patients —that is, many people who suffer—view those who are helping them with fear and apprehension. Doctors, psychiatrists, psychologists, priests, ministers, nurses, social workers are often looked up to by those in need as if they were endowed with a mysterious power. Many patients accept that these professionals can say things that cannot be understood, do things that cannot be questioned and often make decisions about their lives with no explanations. To witness the strange mixture of awe and fear on the faces of many patients, just look in at the many waiting rooms of the different healers. The poor are often most subject to these emotions which only add to their already painful sufferings.

While spending a summer in Bolivia, I discovered that practically all the baptisms I attended were baptisms of dead babies. I was horrified when I noticed that. But then I slowly realized that many people lived so far away from a priest that they hesitated to make the long walk—often more than five hours long—to the church, and did not have their children baptized. But when through illness, accidents or lack of food the baby died, guilt feelings and feelings of fear became so intense that these same people were willing to carry the dead bodies over long distances to ask for baptism before burial. The priests, caught between their conviction that baptism is for the living and not for the dead and their realization that a refusal to baptize only heightens fear and deepens sorrow, tried to help as best they could. But all this reveals how over the ages priests have become in the eyes of many of their own people distant, fearful, powerful men instead of intimate friends and trustworthy servants.

Even in our technically more advanced countries, rectories are seldom experienced as places where you are welcome at any time with any problem. Some people fear priests and ministers; others feel hostile or bitter toward them; many simply don't expect much real help from them; and only very few feel free to knock at their door without uneasiness. In the eyes and feelings of many who suffer, church buildings are perceived more as houses of power than as houses of hospitality. This is true for other professions as well. How many leave hospitals healed of their physical illness but hurt in their feelings by the impersonal treatment they received; how many return from their consultations with psychiatrists, psychologists, social workers or counselors, increasingly irritated by the noncommittal attitude and professional distance they encounter?

But it is easy, too easy indeed, to point an accusing finger at the helping professions. Professionals themselves are often the first to recognize the problem of remaining open and receptive to their patients. In our society technocratic streamlining has depersonalized the interpersonal aspects of the healing professions to a high degree, and increasing demands often force the healer to keep some emotional distance to prevent overinvolvement with his patients.

But still, even in these difficult circumstances, the healer has to keep striving for a spirituality by which interpersonal violence can be prevented and by which the space can be created in which healer and patient can reach out to each other as fellow travelers sharing the same broken human condition.

From the point of view of a Christian spirituality, it is important to stress that every human being is called upon to be a healer. Although there are many professions asking for special long and arduous training, we can never leave the task of healing to the specialist. In fact, the specialists can only retain their humanity in their work when they see their professions as a form of service which they carry out, not instead of, but as part of, the whole people of God. We all are healers who can reach out to offer health, and we all are patients in constant need of help. Only this realization can keep professionals from becoming distant technicians and those in need of care from feeling used or manipulated.

The danger of specialization, therefore, is probably not so much with the specialists as with the nonspecialists, who tend to underestimate their own human potentials and quickly make a referral to those who have titles, thereby leaving their own creative power unused. But when we look at healing as creating space for the stranger, it is clear that all Christians should be willing and able to offer this so much needed form of hospitality.

While teaching at a professional school, I became overwhelmed by the great demand for counseling. Even if there were full-time counselors, they would be so loaded with work that they probably would soon ask for assistance or extra staff. But while living and working with the students for two years, I started to wonder more and more if the students themselves were not hiding their great interpersonal talents. During classroom conversations, at parties and in the context of counseling itself, I started not only to see but also to experience compassion, openness, real interest, a willingness to listen and speak, and many other gifts which seldom became manifest in the student community itself. I suddenly realized that while many complained about loneliness, lack of community or an impersonal atmosphere and expressed a great desire for friendship, support and someone to share experiences with, only a few made their great healing talents visible and available to their fellow students. Fear or a lack of confidence in their own human gift caused many to hide their most precious talents.

We can do much more for each other than we often are aware of. One day Dr. Karl Menninger, the well-known psychiatrist, asked a class of psychiatric residents what the most important part of the treatment process of mental patients was. Some said the psychotherapeutic relationship with the doctor. Some said giving recommendations for future behavior. Others said the prescription of drugs. Others again said the continuing contact with the family after the treatment in the hospital has ended. And there were still different viewpoints. But Karl Menninger did not accept any of these answers as the right one. His answer was "diagnosis." The first and most important task of any healer is making the right diagnosis. Without an accurate diagnosis, subsequent treatment has little effect. Or, to say it better, diagnosis is the beginning of treatment. For Karl Menninger, speaking to a group of future psychiatrists, this obviously

meant that the most attention should be paid to learning
the diagnostic skills of the profession. But when we take
the word diagnosis in its most original and profound
meaning of knowing through and through (*gnosis* =
knowledge; *dia* = through and through), we can see that
the first and most important aspect of all healing is an
interested effort to know the patients fully, in all their
joys and pains, pleasures and sorrows, ups and downs,
highs and lows, which have given shape and form to
their life and have led them through the years to their
present situation. This is far from easy because not only
our own but also other people's pains are hard to face.
Just as we like to reach our own destination through by-
passes, we also like to offer advice, counsel and treatment to others without having really known fully the
wounds that need healing.

But it is exactly in this willingness to know the other
fully that we can really reach out to him or her and become healers. Therefore, healing means, first of all, the
creation of an empty but friendly space where those who
suffer can tell their story to someone who can listen with
real attention. It is sad that often this listening is interpreted as technique. We say, "Give him a chance to talk
it out. It will do him good." And we speak about the
"cathartic" effect of listening, suggesting that "getting it
out of your system" or "getting it out in the open" will
in itself have a purging effect. But listening is an art that
must be developed, not a technique that can be applied
as a monkey wrench to nuts and bolts. It needs the full
and real presence of people to each other. It is indeed one
of the highest forms of hospitality.

Why is listening to know through and through such a
healing service? Because it makes strangers familiar with
the terrain they are traveling through and helps them to
discover the way they want to go. Many of us have lost

our sensitivity for our own history and experience our life as a capricious series of events over which we have no control. When all our attention is drawn away from ourselves and absorbed by what happens around us, we become strangers to ourselves, people without a story to tell or to follow up.

Healing means first of all allowing strangers to become sensitive and obedient to their own stories. Healers, therefore, become students who want to learn, and patients become teachers who want to teach. Just as teachers learn their course material best during the preparation and ordering of their ideas for presentation to students, so patients learn their own story by telling it to a healer who wants to hear it. Healers are hosts who patiently and carefully listen to the story of the suffering strangers. Patients are guests who rediscover their selves by telling their story to the one who offers them a place to stay. In the telling of their stories, strangers befriend not only their host but also their own past.

So healing is the receiving and full understanding of the story so that strangers can recognize in the eyes of their host their own unique way that leads them to the present and suggests the direction in which to go. The story can be hard to tell, full of disappointments and frustrations, full of deviations and stagnations, but it is the only story the stranger has, because it is his own and there will be no hope for the future when the past remains unconfessed, unreceived and misunderstood. Quite often it is our fear for the hidden moments in our own history that keeps us paralyzed.

As healers we have to receive the story of our fellow human beings with a compassionate heart, a heart that does not judge or condemn but recognizes how the stranger's story connects with our own. We have to offer safe boundaries within which the often painful past can be revealed and the search for a new life can find a start.

Our most important question as healers is not, "What to say or to do?" but, "How to develop enough inner space where the story can be received?" Healing is the humble but also very demanding task of creating and offering a friendly empty space where strangers can reflect on their pain and suffering without fear, and find the confidence that makes them look for new ways right in the center of their confusion.

This in no way means that professionally trained healers are less important. The opposite is true. A good host, a careful listener, is the first to recognize when professional help is needed. The many specialists will, in fact, be very grateful to those who have given a compassionate ear to their suffering neighbors, recognized that special care was needed and referred them before their pains grew worse. On the other hand, a general atmosphere of careful attention by all the members of the Christian community can sometimes heal wounds before special care is demanded.

Receptivity and Confrontation

As parents and children, teachers and students, healers and patients, we all reach out to each other in different ways. But in all three types of relationships the concept of hospitality can help us to see that we are called not to own but to serve each other and to create the space where that is possible.

While discussing the three types of relationships in the perspective of hospitality, the emphasis has been on receptivity. Indeed, the stranger has to be received in a free and friendly space where he can reveal his gifts and become our friend. Reaching out to others without being

receptive to them is more harmful than helpful and easily leads to manipulation and even to violence, violence
in thoughts, words and actions. Really honest receptivity
means inviting the stranger into our world on his or her
terms, not on ours. When we say, "You can be my guest
if you believe what I believe, think the way I think and
behave as I do," we offer love under a condition or for a
price. This leads easily to exploitation, making hospitality into a business. In our world in which so many religious convictions, ideologies and life styles come into
increasing contact with each other, it is more important
than ever to realize that it belongs to the essence of a
Christian spirituality to receive our fellow human beings
into our world without imposing our religious viewpoint,
ideology or way of doing things on them as a condition
for love, friendship and care.

We do not have to look far to find these different
viewpoints and attitudes. Often our own children, students or patients have become ideological strangers to us.
Sometimes we feel guilty if we do not at least try to
change their minds or bring them to our side, often to
find out that we only caused suspicion and anger and
made it even more difficult to live together in peace.

But receptivity is only one side of hospitality. The
other side, equally important, is confrontation. To be receptive to the stranger in no way implies that we have to
become neutral "nobodies." Real receptivity asks for
confrontation because space can only be a welcoming
space when there are clear boundaries, and boundaries
are limits between which we define our own position.
Flexible limits, but limits nonetheless. Confrontation results from the articulate presence, the presence within
boundaries, of the host to the guest by which he offers
himself as a point of orientation and a frame of reference. We are not hospitable when we leave our house to

strangers and let them use it any way they want. An empty house is not a hospitable house. In fact, it quickly becomes a ghost house, making the stranger feel uncomfortable. Instead of losing fears, the guest becomes anxious, suspicious of any noise coming from the attic or the cellar. When we want to be really hospitable we not only have to receive strangers but also to confront them by an unambiguous presence, not hiding ourselves behind neutrality but showing our ideas, opinions and life style clearly and distinctly. No real dialogue is possible between somebody and a nobody. We can enter into communication with the other only when our own life choices, attitudes and viewpoints offer the boundaries that challenge strangers to become aware of their own position and to explore it critically.

As a reaction to a very aggressive, manipulative and often degrading type of evangelization, we sometimes have become hesitant to make our own religious convictions known, thereby losing our sense of witness. Although at times it seems better to deepen our own commitments than to evangelize others, it belongs to the core of Christian spirituality to reach out to the other with good news and to speak without embarrassment about what we "have heard and . . . seen with our own eyes . . . watched and touched with our hands" (1 John 1:1).
Receptivity and confrontation are the two inseparable sides of Christian witness. They have to remain in careful balance. Receptivity without confrontation leads to a bland neutrality that serves nobody. Confrontation without receptivity leads to an oppressive aggression which hurts everybody. This balance between receptivity and confrontation is found at different points, depending upon our individual position in life. But in every life situation we not only have to receive but also to confront.

It might be worthwhile to stress at this point that confrontation is much more than "speaking up." Words are seldom the most important form of confrontation. We often have communicated many things long before we speak a word.

I am always fascinated to see how newcomers in my room look around, make comments about the furniture, the paintings and most of all on the books on the shelves. Someone notices the cross on the wall, another makes a remark about an Indian mask; others ask how Freud, Marx and the Bible can be together in one book case. But everyone tries to get a feel of the place just as I do when I enter for the first time someone else's space.

When we have lived a while the walls of our lives have become marked by many events—world events, family events, personal events—as well as by our responses to them. These marks speak their own language and often lead to a dialogue, sometimes limited to the heart, but occasionally expressed in words and gestures. It is in these situations that we reach out to each other and that parents, children, teachers, students, healers, patients and all people meet on their way through life and start speaking to each other and discovering each other as part of a larger community with a common destination.

Chapter 6

HOSPITALITY AND THE HOST

———————————◆┼◆————————————

At Home in Our Own House

The movement from hostility to hospitality cannot be thought of without a constant inner connection with the movement from loneliness to solitude. As long as we are lonely, we cannot be hospitable because as lonely people we cannot create free space. Our own need to still our inner cravings of loneliness makes us cling to others instead of creating space for them.

I vividly remember the story of a student who was invited to stay with a family while studying at a university. After a few weeks he realized how unfree he felt and slowly he became aware that he was becoming the victim of the crying loneliness of his hosts. Husband and wife had become strangers to each other and used their guest to satisfy their great need for affection. The hosts clung to the stranger who had entered their house in the hope that he could offer them the love and intimacy they were unable to give to each other. So the student became entangled in a complex net of unfulfilled needs and desires, and felt caught between the walls of loneliness. He felt the painful tension of having to choose between two lonely partners and was being pulled apart by the cruel question: Are you for him or for me? Are you on her side or on mine? He no longer felt free to go and come when he wanted; he found himself gradually unable to concentrate on his studies while at the same time powerless to offer the help his hosts were begging for. He had even lost the inner freedom to leave.

This story illustrates how difficult it is to create free space for a stranger when there is no solitude in our lives. When we think back to the places where we felt most at home, we quickly see that it was where our hosts gave us the precious freedom to come and go on our own terms and did not claim us for their own needs. Only in a free space can re-creation take place and new life be found. The real host is the one who offers that space where we do not have to be afraid and where we can listen to our own inner voices and find our own personal way of being human. But to be such a host we have to first of all be at home in our own house.

Poverty Makes a Good Host

To the degree in which our loneliness is converted into solitude we can move from hostility to hospitality. There obviously is no question of chronology. The complex and subtle movements of the inner life cannot be neatly divided. But it remains true that loneliness often leads to hostile behavior and that solitude is the climate of hospitality. When we feel lonely we have such a need to be liked and loved that we are hypersensitive to the many signals in our environment and easily become hostile toward anyone whom we perceive as rejecting us. But once we have found the center of our life in our own heart and have accepted our aloneness, not as a fate but as a

vocation, we are able to offer freedom to others. Once we
have given up our desire to be fully fulfilled, we can offer
emptiness to others. Once we have become poor, we can
be a good host. It is indeed the paradox of hospitality
that poverty makes a good host. Poverty is the inner
disposition that allows us to take away our defenses and
convert our enemies into friends. We can only perceive
the stranger as an enemy as long as we have something
to defend. But when we say, "Please enter—my house is
your house, my joy is your joy, my sadness is your sadness and my life is your life," we have nothing to defend,
since we have nothing to lose but all to give.

Turning the other cheek means showing our enemies
that they can only be our enemies while supposing that
we are anxiously clinging to our private property, whatever it is: our knowledge, our good name, our land, our
money, or the many objects we have collected around us.
But who will be our robber when everything he wants to
steal from us becomes our gift to him? Who can lie to us,
when only the truth will serve him well? Who wants to
sneak into our back door, when our front door is wide
open?

Poverty makes a good host. This paradoxical statement
needs some more explanation. In order to be able to
reach out to the other in freedom, two forms of poverty
are very important, the poverty of mind and the poverty
of heart.

The Poverty of Mind

Someone who is filled with ideas, concepts, opinions
and convictions cannot be a good host. There is no inner
space to listen, no openness to discover the gift of the
other. It is not difficult to see how those "who know it
all" can kill a conversation and prevent an interchange of

ideas. Poverty of mind as a spiritual attitude is a growing willingness to recognize the incomprehensibility of the mystery of life. The more mature we become the more we will be able to give up our inclination to grasp, catch, and comprehend the fullness of life and the more we will be ready to let life enter into us.

The preparation for the ministry can offer a good example. To prepare ourselves for service we have to prepare ourselves for an articulate not knowing, a *docta ignorantia,* a learned ignorance. This is very difficult to accept for people whose whole attitude is toward mastering and controlling the world. We all want to be educated so that we can be in control of the situation and make things work according to our own need. But education to ministry is an education not to master God but to be mastered by God.

I remember the educational story of a thirty-year-old Methodist minister from South Africa. When this man felt called to the ministry and was accepted by the church, he was sent as an assistant pastor to work in a parish without any formal theological training. But he was so convinced of his insights and experience, and his enthusiasm and fervor were so great that he had no problem in giving long sermons and strong lectures. But then, after two years, he was called back and sent to the seminary for theological education. Reflecting on his time in the seminary, he said, "During those years I read the works of many theologians, philosophers and novelists. Whereas before everything seemed so clear-cut and self-evident to me, I now lost my certainties, developed many questions and became much less certain of myself and my truth." In a sense, his years of formation were more years of unlearning than of learning and when he returned to the ministry he had less to say but much more to listen to.

This story illustrates that well-educated ministers are not individuals who can tell you exactly who God is, where good and evil are and how to travel from this world to the next, but people whose articulate not-knowing makes them free to listen to the voice of God in the words of the people, in the events of the day and in the books containing the life experience of men and women from other places and other times. In short, learned ignorance makes one able to receive the word from others and the Other with great attention. That is the poverty of mind. It demands the continuing refusal to identify God with any concept, theory, document or event, thus preventing man or woman from becoming a fanatic sectarian or enthusiast, while allowing for an ongoing growth in gentleness and receptivity.

What is true for the ministry is also true for other forms of human service. When we look at the daily life and work of psychiatrists, psychologists, social workers and counselors, we can see how much of their skill consists of a careful listening, with or without instruments, and a continuing concern for not being in the way of their patients. A voluntary poverty of mind makes professionals open to receive constantly new knowledge and insight from those who ask their help. This in no way denies the importance of very concrete and visible help, or the urgency of new structures to alleviate the hunger, thirst, lack of clothes or shelter of millions of people. The contrary is true. When we can work for the poor in a spirit of receptivity and gratitude our help can be accepted without shame. Many people in physical, mental or spiritual need are making it increasingly clear that it is better to refuse help and maintain self-respect than to accept it while being reduced to the status of a beggar or a slave.

The Poverty of Heart

A good host not only has to be poor in mind but also poor in heart. When our heart is filled with prejudices, worries, jealousies, there is little room for a stranger. In a fearful environment it is not easy to keep our hearts open to the wide range of human experiences. Real hospitality, however, is not exclusive but inclusive and creates space for a large variety of human experiences. Also here the ministry can serve as an example of the value of this form of poverty. There are many people who claim to have had a religious experience which showed them the way to God. Frequently, the experience is of such an intensity that it is no longer possible for such a person to realize that his or her way is not necessarily *the* way. Just as God cannot be "caught" or "comprehended" in any specific idea, concept, opinion or conviction, he cannot be defined by any specific feeling or emotion either. God cannot be identified with a good affectionate feeling toward our neighbor, or with a sweet emotion of the heart, or with ecstasies, movements of the body or handling of snakes. God is not just our good inclinations, our fervor, our generosity or our love. All these experiences of the heart may remind us of God's presence, but their absence does not prove God's absence. God is not only greater than our mind, he is also greater than our heart, and just as we have to avoid the temptation of adapting God to our small concepts we also have to avoid adapting him to our small feelings.

Not only in the ministry but in all other helping professions as well we have to remind ourselves constantly that an inflated heart is just as dangerous as an inflated mind. An inflated heart can make us very intolerant. But when we are willing to detach ourselves from making our own limited experience the criterion for our approach to others, we may be able to see that life is greater than our life, history is greater than our history, experience greater than our experience and God greater than our God. That is the poverty of heart that makes a good host. With poverty of heart we can receive the experiences of others as a gift to us. Their histories can creatively connect with ours, their lives give new meaning to ours, and their God speak to ours in mutual revelation.

Johannes Metz describes this disposition well when he writes:

> We must forget ourselves in order to let the other person approach us. We must be able to open up to him to let his distinctive personality unfold—even though it often frightens and repels us. We often keep the other person down, and only see what we want to see; then we never really encounter the mysterious secret of his being, only ourselves. Failing to risk the poverty of encounter, we indulge in a new form of self-assertion and pay the price for it: loneliness. Because we did not risk the poverty of openness (Matthew 10:39), our lives are not graced with the warm fullness of human existence. We are left with only a shadow of our real self.[1]

Poverty of heart creates community since it is not in self-sufficiency but in a creative interdependency that the mystery of life unfolds itself to us.

Boasting of Our Weakness

So hospitality requires poverty, the poverty of mind and the poverty of heart. This might help us to understand the importance of a "training" for hospitality. There are many programs to prepare people for service in its different forms. But seldom do we look at these programs as a training toward a voluntary poverty. Instead we want to become better equipped and more skillful. We want to acquire the "tools of the trade." But real training for service asks for a hard and often painful process of self-emptying. The main problem of service is to be the way without being "in the way." And if there are any tools, techniques and skills to be learned they are primarily to plow the field, to cut the weeds and to clip the branches, that is, to take away the obstacles for real growth and development. Training for service is not a training to become rich but to become voluntarily poor; not to fulfill ourselves but to empty ourselves; not to conquer God but to surrender to his saving power. All this is very hard to accept in our contemporary world, which tells us about the importance of power and influence. But it is important that in this world there remain a few voices crying out that if there is anything to boast of, we should boast of our weakness. Our fulfillment is in offering emptiness, our usefulness in becoming useless, our power in becoming powerless. It indeed belongs to the core of the Christian message that God did not reveal himself to us as the powerful other, unapproachable in his omniscience, omnipotence and omnipresence. Instead he came to us in Jesus Christ who "did not cling to his equality with God, but emptied himself . . . and became as men are; and being as all men are, he was humbler yet, even to accepting death, death on a cross" (Philippians, 2:6–8). It is God himself who reveals to us the movement of our spiritual life. It is not the movement from weakness to power, but the movement in which we become less and less fearful and defensive and more and more open to the other and his world, even when it leads to suffering and death.

While the movement from loneliness to solitude makes us reach out to our innermost self, the movement from hostility to hospitality makes us reach out to others. The term hospitality was used only to come to a better insight into the nature of a mature Christian relationship to our fellow human beings. Words such as creating space, receptivity and confrontation, poverty of mind and heart were used to show that the spirituality of the Christian not only is rooted in the reality of everyday life, but also transcends it by relying on the gift of God. To help, to serve, to care, to guide, to heal, these words were all used to express a reaching out toward our neighbor whereby we perceive life as a gift not to possess but to share.

This finally leads to the most important and difficult aspect of spiritual life, our relationship to him who gives. God has been mentioned already, in fact more and more as we moved from loneliness to solitude and from hostility to hospitality. The emphasis until now, however, was on the question: how to reach out to our innermost self and to our fellow human beings? But can we reach out to God, the source and giver of our own and our neighbor's life? If the answer is no, then solitude and hospitality remain vague ideals good to speak about but unreal in daily life. The movement from illusion to prayer, therefore, is the most crucial movement of the spiritual life undergirding all that has been said thus far.

REACHING OUT TO OUR GOD

The Third Movement:
From Illusion to Prayer

Chapter 7

PRAYER AND MORTALITY

———————————>⊹ ⊹<———————————

A Reality Hard to Touch

Although loneliness and hostility are more easily understandable in light of our day-to-day experiences than the awareness of the illusory quality of many of our strivings, it is only in the lasting effort to unmask the illusions of our existence that a real spiritual life is possible. In order to convert our crying loneliness into a silent solitude and to create a fearless place where strangers can feel at home, we need the willingness and courage to reach out far beyond the limitations of our fragile and finite existence toward our loving God in whom all life is anchored. The silence of solitude is nothing but dead silence when it does not make us alert for a new voice sounding from beyond all human chatter. Hospitality leads only to a congested home when nobody is traveling anywhere.

Solitude and hospitality can only bear lasting fruits when they are embedded in a broader, deeper and higher reality from which they receive their vitality. This reality has been presupposed and here and there touched upon in the description of the first two movements of the spiritual life. But these movements are "first," only in the sense that they are more quickly recognizable and easier to identify with. Not because they are more important. In fact, they could only be described and reflected upon because they are rooted in the most basic movement of the spiritual life, which is the movement from illusion to prayer. It is through this movement that we reach out to God, our God, the one who is eternally real and from whom all reality comes forth. Therefore, the movement from illusion to prayer undergirds and makes possible the movements from loneliness to solitude and from hostility to hospitality and leads us to the core of the spiritual life.

This "first and final" movement is so central to our spiritual life that it is very hard to come in touch with it, to get a grasp on it, to get hold of it, or even—to put a finger on it. Not because this movement is vague or unreal, but because it is so close that it hardly allows the distance needed for articulation and understanding. Maybe this is the reason why the most profound realities of life are the easiest victims of trivialization.

Newspaper interviews with monks who have given their life to prayer in silence and solitude out of a burning love for God, usually boil down to silly stories about changes in regulations and seemingly strange customs. Questions about the "why" of love, marriage, the priesthood or any basic life decision usually lead to meaningless platitudes, a lot of stuttering and shaking of shoulders. Not that these questions are unimportant, but their answers are too deep and too close to our innermost being to be caught in human words.

Maybe we can learn something in this regard from the tightrope walker, Philippe Petit! After being arrested by the police for walking on a rope, which he and his friends had shot from one of the towers of New York's

World Trade Center to the other, he was taken to the city hospital for psychiatric examination. When they found him perfectly sane and in good spirits, they asked: "But why . . . why do you want to walk on a tightrope between the highest towers of the city and risk your life?" Philippe Petit, at first somewhat puzzled by the question, said: "Well . . . if I see three oranges, I have to juggle, and if I see two towers, I have to walk."[1]

That answer says it all. What is most obvious, most close, doesn't need an explanation. Who asks a child why he plays with a ball; who asks a tightrope walker why he walks on his rope—and who asks a lover why he loves?

What is closest to our person is most difficult to express and explain. This is not just true for lovers, artists and tightrope walkers but also for those who pray. While prayer is the expression of a most intimate relationship, it also is the most difficult subject to speak about and becomes easily the subject for trivialities and platitudes. While it is the most human of all human acts, it is also easily perceived as the most superfluous and superstitious activity.

Still, we have to keep speaking about prayer as we keep speaking about love, lovers, art and artists. Because when we do not stay in touch with that center of our spiritual life called prayer, we lose touch with all that grows from it. When we do not enter into that inner field of tension where the movement from illusion to prayer takes place, our solitude and our hospitality easily lose their depth. And then, instead of being essential to our spiritual life, they become pious ornaments of a morally respectable existence.

The Illusion of Immortality

The greatest obstacle to our entering into that profound dimension of life where our prayer takes place is our all-pervasive illusion of immortality. At first it seems unlikely or simply untrue that we have such an illusion, since on many levels we are quite aware of our mortality. Who thinks that he is immortal? But the first two movements of our spiritual life have already revealed to us that things are not quite that simple. Every time we search anxiously for another human being who can break the chains of our loneliness, and every time we build new defenses to protect our life as an inalienable property, we find ourselves caught in that tenacious illusion of immortality. Although we keep telling each other and ourselves that we will not live forever and that we are going to die soon, our daily actions, thoughts and concerns keep revealing to us how hard it is to fully accept the reality of our own statements.

Small, seemingly innocent events keep telling us how easily we eternalize ourselves and our world. It takes only a hostile word to make us feel sad and lonely. It takes only a rejecting gesture to plunge us into self-complaint. It takes only a substantial failure in our work to lead us into a self-destructive depression. Although we have learned from parents, teachers, friends and many books, sacred as well as profane, that we are worth more than what the world makes us, we keep giving an eternal value to the things we own, the people we know, the plans we have, and the successes we "collect." Indeed, it takes only a small disruption to lay our illusion of immortality bare and to reveal how much we have become victimized by our surrounding world suggesting to us that we are "in control." Aren't the many feelings of sadness, heaviness of heart and even dark despair, often intimately connected with the exaggerated seriousness with which we have clothed the people we know, the ideas to which we are exposed and the events we are part of? This lack of distance, which excludes the humor in life, can create a suffocating depression which prevents us from lifting our heads above the horizon of our own limited existence.

Sentimentality and Violence

To come a little closer to our great illusion, it might be helpful to show two of its most visible symptoms: sentimentality and violence. Seemingly quite different forms of behavior, both can be understood, within the perspective of spirituality, as being anchored in the human illusion of immortality.

Sentimentality appears often where intimate relationships become "dead heavy" and people cling to each other with a nearly suicidal seriousness. When we load our fellow human beings with immortal expectations, separation or the threat of it can release uncontrollable sentiments.

In Holland, during a yearly peace march in which 3,000 high school students walk and talk together for three days, the leaders were startled by the renewed sentimentality that characterized the interaction between the marchers. For these, usually quite reserved Dutchmen, holding hands was the most important experience, and the hour of farewell saw a railway station filled with hugging and crying boys and girls. In their reflection after the march, some marchers even wondered how they could ever live happily again after such an experience of communion. While feeling distant from the religious words and gestures of the church which had called them to march, their unique experience of togetherness stirred up powerful and frightening sentiments.

This event illustrates how sentimentality can manifest itself as the result of false expectations of intimate human relationships. This intimacy can lead to depression and despair when it is masked with immortality. When we are not able to look beyond the boundaries of human togetherness and anchor our lives in God, the source of all intimacy, it is hard to cast off the illusion of immortality and be together without being drowned in a pool of sentimentality.

But sentimentality is only one side of the illusion of immortality. Violence is the other. It indeed is not so strange that sentimentality and cruelty are often found in the same people. The image of Hitler, moved to tears by a small child, stands in the memory of many who witnessed his merciless cruelties. The same illusion which in one situation can lead to tears can lead to torture in another situation. The following story shows this in all its consequences.

During the Second World War, a Lutheran bishop, imprisoned in a German concentration camp, was tortured by an S.S. officer who wanted to force him to a confession. In a small room, the two men were facing each other, one afflicting the other with increasing pain. The bishop, who had a remarkable tolerance for pain, did not respond to the torture. His silence, however, enraged the officer to such a degree that he hit his victim harder and harder until he finally exploded and shouted at his victim, "But don't you know that I can kill you?" The bishop looked in the eyes of his torturer and said slowly, "Yes, I know—do what you want—

but I have already died—." At that moment the S.S. officer could no longer raise his arm and lost power over his victim. It was as if he were paralyzed, no longer able to touch him. All his cruelties had been based on the supposition that this man would hold onto his own life as to his most valuable property, and would be quite willing to give his confession in exchange for his life. But with the grounds for his violence gone, torture had become a ridiculous and futile activity.

This story makes it clear that not only sentimentality but also violence is a symptom of the illusion that our lives belong to us. Our human relationships easily become subject to violence and destruction when we treat our own and other people's lives as properties to be defended or conquered and not as gifts to be received. We often see in the center of an intimate relationship the seeds of violence. The borders between kissing and biting, caressing and slapping, hearing and overhearing, looking with tenderness and looking with suspicion are very fragile indeed. When the hidden illusion of immortality becomes dominant in our intimate relationship, it does not take much to turn our desire to be loved into a lustful violence. When our unfulfilled needs lead us to demand from our fellow human beings what they cannot give, we make them into idols and ourselves into devils. By asking for more than a human response we are tempted to behave as less than human. By acting on the illusion that the world belongs to us as private property which nobody ever can take away from us, we become a threat to each other and make intimacy impossible.

To reach a really nonviolent intimacy, we have to unmask our illusion of immortality, fully accept death as our human destiny and reach out beyond the limits of

our existence to our God out of whose intimacy we are
born.

The Idolatry of Our Dreams

But illusions are stronger than we might want them to
be. Although we can say in our waking hours that everything is mortal, that we cannot hold anything forever,
and although we can even develop a deep, inner sense of
the preciousness of life, our night dreams and daydreams
keep creating immortal images. When we feel like a
small child during the day, our frustrated mind is all too
willing to make us into tall and great heroes in our
dreaming moments: into victorious heroes admired by all
those who do not take us so seriously when we are
awake, or into tragic heroes recognized too late by those
who criticized us during our life. In our dreams, we can
become like the first Joseph generously forgiving his
brother in Egypt or, like the second one, carefully carrying his persecuted child to the same land. In our dreams,
we can freely erect statues to honor our own martyrdom
and burn incense for our wounded self. These images
with which we often fill our unfulfilled desires remind us
how quickly we substitute one idol for another. Un-
masking illusions twenty-four hours a day is harder than
we might think.

It would be unwise to try to change our dreams directly or to start worrying about the unexpected images
that appear during our nights. The idols of our dreams,
however, are humbling reminders that we still have a
long way to go before we are ready to meet our God, not
the God created by our own hands or mind, but the un-
created God out of whose loving hands we are born.
Idolatry, which is the worshipping of false gods, is a
temptation much greater than we tend to believe. It will

take much faithfulness and patience to allow not only our conscious but also our unconscious life to move from illusion to prayer.

St. Basil, father of monasticism in the Eastern Orthodox Church, living in the 4th century, was quite clear about the fact that even our dreams cannot be excluded from our spiritual life. When the question was raised to him: "What is the source of those unbecoming nocturnal phantasies?" he said: "They arise out of the disordered movements of the soul that occur during the day. But if a man should occupy himself with the judgments of God and so purify his soul and concern himself constantly with good matters and things pleasing to God, then these things will fill his dreams (instead)."[2]

Although the illusions of our dreams cannot be addressed directly, it indeed is our vocation to reach out to God, not only in our waking hours but in our dreams as well. Patiently but persistently we must slowly unmask the illusions of our immortality, dispelling even the feeble creations of our frustrated mind, and stretch out our arms to the deep sea and the high heaven in a never-ending prayer. When we move from illusion to prayer, we move from the human shelter to the house of God. It is there that our solitude as well as our hospitality can be sustained.

The Hard Questions

This leads to difficult questions: Can we reach out to God as our God? Is intimacy with God possible? Can we develop a loving relationship with him who transcends all our understanding? Is the movement from illusion to prayer anything more than a movement into a vague cloudiness?

These questions are not totally new. They were already present from the moment the first lines of a spiritual life were drawn. Reaching out to our innermost self was not just a reaching out to more of ourselves, to more detailed understanding of our inner complexities. No, it was indeed a reaching to a center where a new encounter could take place, where we could reach beyond our selves to him who speaks in our solitude. Reaching out to strangers was not just a reaching out to the long row of people who are so obviously needy—in need of food, clothing and of many forms of care—but also a reaching out to the promises they are bringing with them as gifts to their host. All that has been said about solitude and hospitality points to someone higher than our thoughts can reach, someone deeper than our hearts can feel and wider than our arms can embrace, someone under whose wings we can find refuge (Psalm 90) and in whose love we can rest, someone we call our God.

But although the questions about our relationship to God, our God, are not totally new, now they are raised more directly, more confrontingly, more drastically. At some point we all feel that solitude and hospitality are good things to strive for and reflect upon. They have some obvious human value, and few people will deny that they are elements of a mature existence, certainly when they are kept in balance. But prayer? The claim that prayer as a loving intimacy with God is the ground in which solitude and hospitality are rooted, that claim tends to lead to embarrassment. Many will say, "Well—I could follow you so far, but here you are on your own." And why should they feel differently? Don't we use the word prayer mostly when we feel that our human limits are reached? Isn't the word prayer more a word to indicate powerlessness rather than a creative contact with the source of all life?

It is important to say that these feelings, experiences, questions and irritations about prayer are very real and often the result of concrete and painful events. Still, a spiritual life without prayer is like the gospel without Christ. Instead of proving or defending anything, it might be worthwhile to simply bring all the doubtful and anxious questions together in this one question: "If prayer, understood as an intimate relationship with God, is indeed the basis of all relationships—to ourselves as well as to others—how then can we learn to pray and really experience prayer as the axis of our existence?" By focusing on this question, it becomes possible to explore the importance of prayer in our own lives and in the lives of those we have met through personal encounters or through stories and books.

The Paradox of Prayer

The paradox of prayer is that we have to learn how to pray while we can only receive it as a gift. It is exactly this paradox that clarifies why prayer is the subject of so many seemingly contrasting statements.

All the great saints in history and all the spiritual directors worth their salt say that we have to learn to pray, since prayer is our first obligation as well as our highest calling. Libraries have been written about the question of how to pray. Many men and women have tried to articulate the different forms and levels of their impressive experiences, and have encouraged their readers to follow their road. They remind us repeatedly of St. Paul's words: "Pray constantly" (1 Thessalonians 5:17), and often give elaborate instructions on how to develop an intimate relationship with God. We even find different "schools of prayer," and, not surprisingly, elaborate arguments in favor of one school or another.

One such school or tradition is Hesychasm (from the Greek word *hēsychia* = repose). Theophan the Recluse, a nineteenth-century Russian Hesychast, offers a beautiful example of an instruction in prayer when he writes:

> Make yourself a rule always to be with the Lord, keeping your mind in your heart and do not let your thoughts wander; as often as they stray, turn them back again and keep them at home in the closet of your heart and delight in converse with the Lord.[3]

There is no doubt that Theophan, and with him all great spiritual writers, consider a serious discipline essential to arriving at an intimate relationship with God. For them, prayer, without a continuous and arduous effort, is not worth talking about. In fact, some spiritual writers have written down their efforts to pray in such concrete and vivid details that they often leave the reader with the erroneous impression that you can reach any level of prayer by just hard work and stern perseverance. This impression has created many disillusions since many felt, after long years of strenuous "prayer work," that they were farther away from God than when they started.

But the same saints and spiritual guides, who speak about the discipline of prayer, also keep reminding us that prayer is a gift of God. They say that we cannot truly pray by ourselves, but that it is God's spirit who prays in us. St. Paul put it very clearly: "No one can say, 'Jesus is Lord' unless he is under the influence of the Holy Spirit" (1 Corinthians 12:3). We cannot force God into a relationship. God comes to us on his own initiative, and no discipline, effort, or ascetic practice can make him come. All mystics stress with an impressive unanimity that prayer is "grace," that is, a free gift from

God, to which we can only respond with gratitude. But they hasten to add that this precious gift indeed is within our reach. In Jesus Christ, God has entered into our lives in the most intimate way, so that we could enter into his life through the Spirit. That is the meaning of the powerful words Jesus spoke to his apostles on the evening before his death: "I must tell you the truth: it is for your own good that I am going because unless I go, the Advocate [= the Spirit] will not come to you; but if I do go, I will send him to you" (John 16:7). In Jesus, God became one of us to lead us through Jesus into the intimacy of his divine life. Jesus came to us to become as we are and left us to allow us to become as he is. By giving us his Spirit, his breath, he became closer to us than we are to ourselves. It is through this breath of God that we can call God "Abba, Father" and can become part of the mysterious divine relationship between Father and Son. Praying in the Spirit of Jesus Christ, therefore, means participating in the intimate life of God himself.

Thomas Merton writes:

> The union of the Christian with Christ . . . is a mystical union in which Christ Himself becomes the source and principle of life in me. Christ Himself . . . "breathes" in me divinely in giving me His Spirit.[4]

There is probably no image that expresses so well the intimacy with God in prayer as the image of God's breath. We are like asthmatic people who are cured of their anxiety. The Spirit has taken away our narrowness (the Latin word for anxiety is *angustia* = narrowness) and made everything new for us. We receive a new breath, a new freedom, a new life. This new life is the divine life of God himself. Prayer, therefore, is God's breathing in us, by which we become part of the intimacy of God's inner life, and by which we are born anew.

So, the paradox of prayer is that it asks for a serious effort while it can only be received as a gift. We cannot plan, organize or manipulate God; but without a careful discipline, we cannot receive him either. This paradox of prayer forces us to look beyond the limits of our mortal existence. To the degree that we have been able to dispel our illusion of immortality and have come to the full realization of our fragile mortal condition, we can reach out in freedom to the creator and re-creator of life and respond to his gifts with gratitude.

Prayer is often considered a weakness, a support system, which is used when we can no longer help ourselves. But this is only true when the God of our prayers is created in our own image and adapted to our own needs and concerns. When, however, prayer makes us reach out to God, not on our own but on his terms, then prayer pulls us away from self-preoccupations, encourages us to leave familiar ground, and challenges us to enter into a new world which cannot be contained within the narrow boundaries of our mind or heart. Prayer, therefore, is a great adventure because the God with whom we enter into a new relationship is greater than we are and defies all our calculations and predictions. The movement from illusion to prayer is hard to make since it leads us from false certainties to true uncertainties, from an easy support system to a risky surrender, and from the many "safe" gods to the God whose love has no limits.

The Absence and Presence of God

God is "beyond," beyond our heart and mind, beyond our feelings and thoughts, beyond our expectations and desires, and beyond all the events and experiences that

make up our life. Still he is in the center of all of it. Here
we touch the heart of prayer since here it becomes manifest that in prayer the distinction between God's presence and God's absence no longer really distinguishes. In
prayer, God's presence is never separated from his absence and God's absence is never separated from his
presence. His presence is so much beyond the human
experience of being together that it quite easily is perceived as absence. His absence, on the other hand, is
often so deeply felt that it leads to a new sense of his
presence. This is powerfully expressed in Psalm 22:1–5:

> My God, my God, why have you deserted me?
> How far from saving me, the words I groan!
> I call all day, my God, but you never answer,
> all night long I call and cannot rest.
> Yet, Holy One, you
> who make your home in the praises of Israel,
> in you our fathers put their trust,
> they trusted and you rescued them;
> they called to you for help and they were saved,
> they never trusted you in vain.

This prayer not only is the expression of the experience
of the people of Israel, but also the culmination of the
Christian experience. When Jesus spoke these words on
the cross, total aloneness and full acceptance touched
each other. In that moment of complete emptiness all
was fulfilled. In that hour of darkness new light was
seen. While death was witnessed, life was affirmed.
Where God's absence was most loudly expressed, his
presence was most profoundly revealed.

When God himself in his humanity became part of our
most painful experience of God's absence, he became
most present to us. It is in this mystery that we enter
when we pray. The intimacy with God in our earthly

existence will always remain an intimacy that transcends human intimacy and is experienced in a faithful waiting on him who came but is still to come. Although at exceptional moments we may be overwhelmed by a deep sense of God's presence in the center of our solitude and in the midst of the space we create for others, more often than not we are left with the painful sense of emptiness and can only experience God as the absent God.

The French author Simone Weil writes in her notebooks: "Waiting patiently in expectation is the foundation of the spiritual life."[5] With these words she expresses powerfully how absence and presence are never separated when we reach out to God in prayer. The spiritual life is, first of all, a patient waiting, that is, a waiting in suffering *(patior = to suffer)*, during which the many experiences of unfulfillment remind us of God's absence. But it also is a waiting in expectation which allows us to recognize the first signs of the coming God in the center of our pains. The mystery of God's presence, therefore, can be touched only by a deep awareness of his absence. It is in the center of our longing for the absent God that we discover his footprints, and realize that our desire to love God is born out of the love with which he has touched us. In the patient waiting for the loved one, we discover how much he has filled our lives already. Just as the love of a mother for her son can grow deeper when he is far away, just as children can learn to appreciate their parents more when they have left the home, just as lovers can rediscover each other during long periods of absence, so our intimate relationship with God can become deeper and more mature by the purifying experience of his absence. By listening to our longings, we hear God as their creator. By touching the center of our solitude, we sense that we have been touched by loving hands. By watching carefully our endless desire to love, we come to the growing awareness that we can love only because we have been loved first, and that we can offer intimacy only because we are born out of the inner intimacy of God himself.

In our violent times, in which destruction of life is so rampant and the raw wounds of humanity so visible, it is very hard to tolerate the experience of God as a purifying absence, and to keep our hearts open so as to patiently and reverently prepare his way. We are tempted to grasp rapid solutions instead of inquiring about the validity of the questions. Our inclination to put faith in any suggestion that promises quick healing is so great that it is not surprising that spiritual experiences are mushrooming all over the place and have become highly sought after commercial items. Many people flock to places and persons who promise intensive experiences of togetherness, cathartic emotions of exhilaration and sweetness, and liberating sensations of rapture and ecstasy. In our desperate need for fulfillment and our restless search for the experience of divine intimacy, we are all too prone to construct our own spiritual events. In our impatient culture, it has indeed become extremely difficult to see much salvation in waiting.

But still . . . the God who saves is not made by human hands. He transcends our psychological distinctions between "already" and "not yet," absence and presence, leaving and returning. Only in a patient waiting in expectation, can we slowly break away from our illusions and pray as the psalmist prayed.

> God, you are my God, I am seeking you,
> my soul is thirsting for you,
> my flesh is longing for you,
> a land parched, weary and waterless;

I long to gaze on you in the Sanctuary,
and to see your power and glory.

Your love is better than life itself,
my lips will recite your praise;
all my life I will bless you,
in your name lift up my hands;
my soul will feast most richly,
on my lips a song of joy and, in my mouth, praise.

On my bed I think of you,
I meditate on you all night long,
for you have always helped me.
I sing for joy in the shadow of your wings;
my soul clings close to you,
your right hand supports me.
(Psalm 63:1–8)

Converting Protest into Prayer

When we can cast off our illusions of immortality we
can create the open-ended space in which we can stretch
out our arms to our God, who transcends all our expectations, dreams and desires. We will probably never be
fully free from illusions, just as we will never be fully
free from loneliness and hostility. But when we recognize our illusions as illusions, we also will recognize the
first outlines of prayer. We are always on the move between the two poles of illusion and prayer. There are
times when our daily work absorbs us so fully that the
word "prayer" only evokes irritation. There also are
times when prayer seems easy, obvious and nearly another word for living. But usually we find ourselves
somewhere in-between; praying while holding on with
at least one hand to our cherished belongings, only
vaguely aware of their illusory quality.

At some times, however, we are forced again to
awaken from this half-asleep-half-awake state. When in

a crisis of war, sudden poverty, illness or death we are confronted with the "absurdities of life," we can no longer remain neutral and are asked to respond. Often our first and most visible response is a protest bursting forth from our bewilderment. It is at these crucial moments of life that we are reminded again of our illusions and asked to convert our protest into prayer. This is a very hard task, but a task leading us not away from reality but closer to it.

Recently a student who had just finished his long studies for the ministry and was ready to start in his first church suddenly died after a fatal fall from his bike. Those who knew him well felt a strong, angry protest arising from their hearts. Why him, a very noble man who could have done so much for so many? Why now, just when his long, costly education could start bearing fruit? Why in this way, so unprepared and unheroic? There were no answers to all these reasonable questions. A strong angry protest seemed the only human response.

But such a protest is the continuation of our illusion that we know what life is all about, that we rule it and determine its values as well as its goals. We do not and are challenged instead to convert our protest against the absurdities of the human existence into a prayer lifting us beyond the boundaries of our existence to him who holds our life in his hands and heart with boundless love and mercy. In our attempts to accept this challenge, we are wise to say to ourselves with the words of the psalmist:

You men, why shut your hearts so long,
loving delusions, chasing after lies.
Know this, Yahweh works wonders for those he loves,
Yahweh hears me when I call to him.
(Psalm 4:2–3)

Chapter 8

THE PRAYER OF THE HEART

————————>╂ ╂⊂————————

The Search for the Fitting Way

Just as there are many ways to be hospitable, there are
many ways to pray. When we are serious about prayer
and no longer consider it one of the many things people
do in their life but, rather, the basic receptive attitude
out of which all of life can receive new vitality, we will,
sooner or later, raise the question: "What is *my* way to
pray, what is the prayer of my heart?" Just as artists
search for the style that is most their own, so people who
pray search for the prayer of their heart. What is most
profound in life, and therefore most dear to us, always
needs to be properly protected as well as expressed. It,
therefore, is not surprising that prayer is often surrounded by carefully prescribed gestures and words, by
detailed rituals and elaborate ceremonies.

A visit to a Trappist monastery can help us realize how
those who have made themselves free for a life exclu-
sively dedicated to prayer subject themselves to a very
strict discipline. The Trappist monk lives his whole
life, day and night, in obedience to St. Benedict's rule,
the holy rule, which is safe-guarded and interpreted
with utmost consideration and discretion by the Ab-

bot, the spiritual father of the community. The holy rule is for the prayer life of a Trappist monk like a golden setting for a precious stone. The rule makes the real beauty of prayer visible and allows it to be fully enjoyed. Neglect of the rule means neglect of prayer. The monk who wants to make his whole life, whatever he does, a continuing prayer knows that this is only possible in the context of a very concrete daily schedule that supports him in the realization of his goal. Therefore, we find that in a Trappist monastery, the celebration of the Eucharist, the communal psalmody, the individual meditation, study and manual work, eating and sleeping are all subject to careful regulation and conscientious observance. Anyone who participates in such a life, if only for a few days, can sense the great mystery of prayer that is hidden, as well as visible, in the deep rhythm of the contemplative day.

This little excursion to the Trappists serves to illustrate the fact that no one who seriously wants to live a life of prayer can persevere in that desire and realize it to some degree without a very concrete way. It may be necessary to make many changes in direction and to explore new ways as life develops, but without any way we won't arrive anywhere.

To come to an answer to the personal question: "What is the prayer of my heart?" we first of all have to know how to find this most personal prayer. Where do we look, what do we do, to whom do we go in order to discover how we as individual human beings—with our own history, our own milieu, our own character, our own insights and our own freedom to act—are called to enter into intimacy with God? The question about the prayer of our heart is, in fact, the question about our own most personal vocation.

Words, Silence and a Guide

It seems possible to establish a few guidelines. A careful look at the lives of people for whom prayer was indeed "the only thing needed" (see Luke 10:42) shows that three "rules" are always observed: a contemplative reading of the word of God, a silent listening to the voice of God, and a trusting obedience to a spiritual guide. Without the Bible, without silent time and without someone to direct us, finding our own way to God is very hard and practically impossible.

In the first place, we have to pay careful attention to the word of God as it is written in the holy scriptures. St. Augustine was converted when he responded to the words of a child saying: "take and read, take and read."[1] When he took the Bible and started reading the page on which he opened it, he felt that the words he read were directly spoken to him.

To take the holy scriptures and read them is the first thing we have to do to open ourselves to God's call. Reading the scriptures is not as easy as it seems since in our academic world we tend to make anything and everything we read subject to analysis and discussion. But the word of God should lead us first of all to contemplation and meditation. Instead of taking the words apart, we should bring them together in our innermost being; instead of wondering if we agree or disagree, we should wonder which words are directly spoken to us and connect directly with our most personal story. Instead of thinking about the words as potential subjects for an interesting dialogue or paper, we should be willing to let them penetrate into the most hidden corners of our

heart, even to those places where no other word has yet
found entrance. Then and only then can the word bear
fruit as seed sown in rich soil. Only then can we really
"hear and understand" (Matthew 13:23).

Secondly, we simply need quiet time in the presence of
God. Although we want to make all our time, time for
God, we will never succeed if we do not reserve a min-
ute, an hour, a morning, a day, a week, a month or whatever period of time for God and him alone. This asks for
much discipline and risk taking because we always seem
to have something more urgent to do and "just sitting
there" and "doing nothing" often disturbs us more than
it helps. But there is no way around this. Being useless
and silent in the presence of our God belongs to the core
of all prayer. In the beginning we often hear our own
unruly inner noises more loudly than God's voice. This is
at times very hard to tolerate. But slowly, very slowly,
we discover that the silent time makes us quiet and
deepens our awareness of ourselves and God. Then, very
soon, we start missing these moments when we are de-
prived of them, and before we are fully aware of it an
inner momentum has developed that draws us more and
more into silence and closer to that still point where God
speaks to us.

Contemplative reading of the holy scriptures and silent time in the presence of God belong closely together.
The word of God draws us into silence; silence makes us
attentive to God's word. The word of God penetrates
through the thick of human verbosity to the silent center
of our heart; silence opens in us the space where the
word can be heard. Without reading the word, silence
becomes stale, and without silence, the word loses its re-
creative power. The word leads to silence and silence to
the word. The word is born in silence, and silence is the
deepest response to the word.

But word and silence both need guidance. How do we know that we are not deluding ourselves, that we are not selecting those words that best fit our passions, that we are not just listening to the voice of our own imagination? Many have quoted the scriptures and many have heard voices and seen visions in silence, but only few have found their way to God. Who can be the judge in his own case? Who can determine if his feelings and insights are leading him in the right direction? Our God is greater than our own heart and mind, and too easily we are tempted to make our heart's desires and our mind's speculations into the will of God. Therefore, we need a guide, a director, a counselor who helps us to distinguish between the voice of God and all the other voices coming from our own confusion or from dark powers far beyond our control. We need someone who encourages us when we are tempted to give it all up, to forget it all, to just walk away in despair. We need someone who discourages us when we move too rashly in unclear directions or hurry proudly to a nebulous goal. We need someone who can suggest to us when to read and when to be silent, which words to reflect upon and what to do when silence creates much fear and little peace.

The first and nearly spontaneous reaction to the idea of a spiritual guide is: "Spiritual guides are hard to find." This might be true, but at least part of the reason for this lack of spiritual guides is that we ourselves do not appeal to our fellow human beings in such a way as to invite them to become our spiritual leaders. If there were no students constantly asking for good teachers, there would be no good teachers. The same is true for spiritual guides. There are many men and women with great spiritual sensitivity whose talents remain dormant because we do not make an appeal to them. Many would, in fact, become wise and holy for our sake if we would invite them to assist us in our search for the prayer of our heart. A spiritual director does not necessarily have to be more intelligent or more experienced than we are. It is important that he or she accepts our invitation to lead us closer to God and enters with us into the scriptures and the silence where God speaks to both of us. When we really want to live a life of prayer and seriously ask ourselves what the prayer of our heart may be, we also will be able to express the type of guidance we need and find that someone is waiting to be asked. Often we will discover that those whom we ask for help will indeed receive the gift to help us and grow with us toward prayer.

Thus, the Bible, silence and a spiritual director are three important guides in our search for our most personal way to enter into an intimate relationship with God. When we contemplate the scriptures continuously, set some time aside to be silent in the presence of our God and are willing to submit our experiences with word and silence to a spiritual guide, we can keep ourselves from developing new illusions and open the way to the prayer of our heart.

The Wisdom of History

Although practically all Christians who want to reach out to their God with faithful perseverance will look at some point in their life for someone who can be their guide, spiritual guidance is not limited to the one-to-one relationship. The spiritual wisdom of many Christians, who in the course of history have dedicated their lives to prayer, is preserved and relived in the different traditions, life styles or spiritualities that remain visible in contemporary Christianity. In fact, our first and most influential guides are often the prayer customs, styles of worship and modes of speaking about God that pervade

our different milieux. Each spiritual milieu has its own
emphasis. Here silence is stressed, there study of the
scriptures; here individual meditation is central, there
communal worship; here poverty is the unifying concept,
there it is obedience; here the great mystical experiences
are suggested as the way to perfection, there the little
way of common daily life. Much of the emphasis depends on the time in which a new spirituality found its
beginning, on the personal character of the man or
woman who was or is its main inspiration and on the
particular needs to which it responds.

The fact that these spiritualities are mostly related to
influential historical personalities with great visibility
helps us to use them as real guides in the search for our
own personal way. Benedict, Francis, Dominic, Ignatius
of Loyola, Teresa of Avila, Jacob Boehme, Francis de
Sales, George Fox, John Wesley, Henry Martyn, John
Henry Newman, Sören Kierkegaard, Charles de Fou-
cauld, Dag Hammarskjöld, Martin Luther King, Jr.,
Thomas Merton and many, many others offer us, by
their own lives and the lives of their disciples and faithful students, a frame of reference and a point of orientation in our attempts to find the prayer of our heart.

I remember meeting one day a very shy, somewhat
withdrawn man. Although he was very intelligent, it
seemed as if the world was just too big for him. Any
suggestion that he do something outstanding or special
scared him. For him, the little way, the conscientious
living of the small realities of everyday life was the
way of prayer. When he spoke about the little Thérèse
of Lisieux, his spiritual guide, his eyes lit up and he
looked full of joy. But his more passionate neighbor
needed the example of Anthony of the Desert or Ber-

nard of Clairvaux and other great spiritual athletes to
help him in his search for an authentic spiritual life.

Without such inspiring guides, it is very difficult to
remain faithful to the desire to find our own way. It is a
hard and often lonely search and we constantly need
new insights, support and comfort to persevere. The really great saints of history don't ask for imitation. Their
way was unique and cannot be repeated. But they invite
us into their lives and offer a hospitable space for our
own search. Some turn us off and make us feel uneasy;
others even irritate us, but among the many great spiritual men and women in history we may find a few, or
maybe just one or two, who speak the language of our
heart and give us courage. These are our guides. Not to
be imitated but to help us live our lives just as authenti-
cally as they lived theirs. When we have found such
guides we have good reason to be grateful and even better reasons to listen attentively to what they have to say.

The Way of a Pilgrim

Among the many spiritualities, styles of prayer and
ways to God, there is one way that is relatively unknown
but might prove to have special relevance in our contemporary spiritual climate. That is the spirituality of
Hesychasm, one of the oldest spiritual traditions in the
Eastern Orthodox Church, which lately received new attention in the West through the publication of an English
edition of *The Way of a Pilgrim.*[2] Rather than giving short
descriptions of different spiritual ways, it seems more
valuable to discuss in some detail just one way: the way
of the Hesychasts. This is valuable not only because
Hesychasm illustrates much that has been said but also
because what it says has a remarkably modern ring to it.

While all of us are called to search with diligence and perseverance for the prayer of our own heart—i.e., the prayer that is most our own and that forms our unique way of reaching out to our God—Hesychasm makes the prayer of the heart its central concept, gives it a very concrete content and offers explicit guidelines to realize it.

What, then is Hesychasm? Hesychasm (from the Greek word *hēsychia*=repose) is a spiritual tradition that found its beginnings in the fifth century, developed in the monasteries on Mount Sinai and later on Mount Athos, was found very much alive during the spiritual renewal in nineteenth-century Russia, and is gradually being discovered by the West as one of the most valuable "schools" of prayer. The prayer in which the hesychastic tradition finds its deepest expression is the Jesus prayer consisting of the simple words: "Lord Jesus Christ, have mercy upon me." Timothy Ware says concerning the Jesus prayer:

> . . . around these few words many Orthodox over the centuries have built their spiritual life and through this one prayer they have entered into the deepest mysteries of Christian knowledge.[3]

There is probably no simpler nor livelier way to understand the richness of Hesychasm and the Jesus prayer than by listening to the remarkable story of an anonymous Russian peasant who wandered through his vast country discovering with growing amazement and inner joy the marvelous fruits of the Jesus prayer. In *The Way of a Pilgrim* his story is written down, most probably by a Russian monk whom he met on his journey.

A few years ago I spent three days in retreat with two close friends. Most of the time we kept silence but after dinner we read to each other the story of the pilgrim. To our own surprise this pleasant and charming spiritual book had a profound influence on us and opened for us a new and very simple way to pray in the midst of our very restless and hectic lives. We still talk about those days as "the days with the pilgrim."

In *The Way of a Pilgrim* the Russian peasant tells us how he goes from town to town, church to church and monk to monk to find out how to pray without ceasing (see 1 Thessalonians 5:17). After having heard many sermons and consulted many people in vain, he finds a holy starets (monk) who teaches him the Jesus prayer. The starets first reads to him the following words of Simeon the New Theologian:

> Sit down alone and in silence. Lower your head, shut your eyes, breathe out gently and imagine yourself looking into your own heart. Carry your mind, i.e., your thoughts, from your head to your heart. As you breathe out say: "Lord Jesus Christ, have mercy on me." Say it moving your lips gently, or say it in your mind. Try to put all other thought aside. Be calm, be patient and repeat the process very frequently.[4]

After having read this to his visitor, the starets instructs him to say the Jesus prayer three thousand times each day, then six thousand times, then twelve thousand times and finally—as often as he wants. The pilgrim is very happy to have found a master and follows carefully his instructions. He says:

> Under this guidance I spent the whole summer in ceaseless oral prayer to Jesus Christ, and I felt absolute peace in my soul. During sleep I often dreamed that I was saying the Prayer. And during the day, if I happened to meet anyone, all men without exception were

as dear to me as if they had been my nearest relations.
. . . I thought of nothing whatever but my Prayer, my
mind tended to listen to it, and my heart began of
itself to feel at times a certain warmth and pleasure.[5]

After the death of his holy starets, the peasant wan-
ders from town to town with his prayer. The prayer has
given him new strength to deal with all the adversities of
the pilgrim life and turns all pains into joy:

At times I do as much as forty-three or -four miles a
day, and do not feel that I am walking at all. I am
aware only of the fact that I am saying my Prayer.
When the bitter cold pierces me, I begin to say my
Prayer more earnestly and I quickly get warm all over.
When hunger begins to overcome me, I call more often
on the Name of Jesus and I forget my wish for food.
When I fall ill and get rheumatism in my back and
legs, I fix my thoughts on the Prayer and do not notice
the pain. If anyone harms me, I have only to think,
"How sweet is the Prayer of Jesus!" and the injury and
the anger alike pass away and I forget it all.[6]

The pilgrim, however, has no illusions. He realizes
that, notwithstanding these events, his prayer had not
yet become the prayer of the heart in the fullest sense.
The starets had told him that all these experiences are
part of "an artificial state which follows quite naturally
upon routine."[7] For the prayer of the heart, he says, "I
await God's time." After many unsuccessful attempts to
find work and a place to stay, he decides to go to the
tomb of St. Innocent of Irkutsk in Siberia.

My idea was that in the forests and steppes of Siberia I
should travel in greater silence and therefore in a way
that was better for prayer and reading. And this jour-

ney I undertook, all the while saying my oral Prayer
without stopping.[8]

It is on this journey that the pilgrim experiences the
prayer of the heart for the first time. In very lively, simple and direct words he tells us how it came about and
how it led him into the most intimate relationship with
Jesus.

> After no great lapse of time I had the feeling that the
> Prayer had, so to speak, by its own action passed from
> my lips to my heart. That is to say, it seemed as
> though my heart in its ordinary beating began to say
> the words of the Prayer within at each beat. . . . I
> gave up saying the Prayer with my lips. I simply lis-
> tened carefully to what my heart was saying. It seemed
> as though my eyes looked right down into it; . . .
> Then I felt something like a pain in my heart, and in
> my thoughts so great a love for Jesus Christ that I
> pictured myself, if only I could see Him, throwing my-
> self at His feet and not letting them go from my em-
> brace, kissing them tenderly, and thanking Him with
> tears for having of His love and grace allowed me to
> find so great a consolation in His Name, me, His un-
> worthy and sinful creature! Further there came into my
> heart a gracious warmth which spread through my
> whole breast.[9]

The prayer of the heart gives the pilgrim an immense
joy and an unspeakable experience of God's presence.
Wherever he goes and with whomever he speaks from
here on, he cannot resist speaking about God who dwells
in him. Although he never tries to convert people or
change their behavior but always looks for silence and
solitude, he nevertheless finds that the people he meets
respond deeply to him and his words and rediscover God

in their own lives. Thus, the pilgrim, who by his confession of sin and unceasing supplication for mercy, recognizes his distance from God, finds himself traveling through the world in his most intimate company and inviting others to share in it.

With the Mind in the Heart

If we should not move beyond the charming story of the Russian peasant and are only enamored by the appeal of its nineteenth-century romanticism, it might lead us no farther than it did Franny and Zooey in J. D. Salinger's novel, that is, to mental confusion.[10]

The pilgrim's story, however, is just one ripple of the deep mystical stream of Russian Hesychasm in the nineteenth century. How deep and powerful this stream really was is revealed in *The Art of Prayer.* This book, which was one of Thomas Merton's favorite books, is an orthodox anthology on the prayer of the heart, collected by Chariton of Valams, and contains excerpts of the works of nineteenth-century Russian spiritual writers, in particular, Bishop Theophan the Recluse. It is a rich record of mystical prayer and shows us one of the most concrete ways to reach out to God from the center of our innermost self. There we hear Theophan the Recluse say to one of the many who asked his guidance:

I will remind you of only one thing: one must descend with the mind into the heart, and there stand before the face of the Lord, ever present, all seeing within you. The prayer takes a firm and steadfast hold, when a small fire begins to burn in the heart. Try not to quench this fire, and it will become established in such a way that the prayer repeats itself: and then you will have within you a small murmuring stream.[11]

To stand in the presence of God with our mind in our heart, that is the essence of the prayer of the heart. Theophan expresses in a very succinct way that the prayer of the heart unifies our whole person and places us without any reservation, mind in heart, in the awesome and loving presence of our God.

If prayer were just an intelligent exercise of our mind, we would soon become stranded in fruitless and trivial inner debates with God. If, on the other hand, prayer would involve only our heart, we might soon think that good prayers consist in good feelings. But the prayer of the heart in the most profound sense unites mind and heart in the intimacy of the divine love.

It is about this prayer that the pilgrim speaks, thereby expressing in his own charming naïve style the profound wisdom of the spiritual fathers of his time. In the expression "Lord Jesus Christ, have mercy upon me," we find a powerful summary of all prayer. It directs itself to Jesus, the son of God, who lived, died and was raised for us; it declares him to be the Christ, the anointed one, the Messiah, the one we have been waiting for; it calls him our Lord, the Lord of our whole being: body, mind and spirit, thought, emotions and actions; and it professes our deepest relationship to him by a confession of our sinfulness and by a humble plea for his forgiveness, mercy, compassion, love and tenderness.[12]

The prayer of the heart can be a special guide to the present-day Christian searching for his own personal way to an intimate relationship to God. More than ever we feel like wandering strangers in a fast-changing world. But we do not want to escape this world. Instead, we want to be fully part of it without drowning in its stormy waters. We want to be alert and receptive to all that happens around us without being paralyzed by inner fragmentation. We want to travel with open eyes through this valley of tears without losing contact with him who calls us to a new land. We want to respond with compassion to all those whom we meet on our way and ask for a hospitable place to stay while remaining solidly rooted in the intimate love of our God.

The prayer of the heart shows us one possible way. It is indeed like a murmuring stream that continues underneath the many waves of every day and opens the possibility of living in the world without being of it and of reaching out to our God from the center of our solitude.

At Home While Still on the Way

The prayer of the heart requires first of all that we make God our only thought. That means that we must dispel all distractions, concerns, worries and preoccupations, and fill the mind with God alone. The Jesus prayer, or any other prayer form, is meant to be a help to gently empty our minds from all that is not God, and offer all the room to him and him alone. But that is not all. Our prayer becomes a prayer of the heart when we have localized in the center of our inner being the empty space in which our God-filled mind can descend and vanish, and where the distinctions between thinking and feeling, knowing and experiencing, ideas and emotions are transcended, and where God can become our host. "The Kingdom of God is within you" (Luke 17:21), Jesus said. The prayer of the heart takes these words seriously. When we empty our mind from all thoughts and our heart from all experiences, we can prepare in the center of our innermost being the home for the God who wants to dwell in us. Then we can say with St. Paul, "I live now not with my own life but with the life of Christ who lives in me" (Galatians 2:20). Then we can affirm Luther's words, "Grace is the experience of being deliv-

ered from experience." And then we can realize that it is
not we who pray, but the Spirit of God who prays in us.

One of the early Fathers said: "When thieves approach
a house in order to creep up to it and steal, and hear
someone inside talking, they do not dare to climb in; in
the same way, when our enemies try to steal into the
soul and take possession of it they creep all round but
fear to enter when they hear that . . . prayer welling
out.[13]

When our heart belongs to God, the world and its
powers cannot steal it from us. When God has become
the Lord of our heart, our basic alienation is overcome
and we can pray with the psalmist:

It was you who created my inmost self,
and put me together in my mother's womb;
for all these mysteries I thank you:
for the wonder of myself, for the wonder of your works.
(Psalm 139:13-14)

When God has become our shepherd, our refuge, our
fortress, then we can reach out to him in the midst of a
broken world and feel at home while still on the way.
When God dwells in us, we can enter in a wordless dialogue with him while still waiting on the day that he will
lead us into the house where he has prepared a place for
us (John 14:2). Then we can wait while we have already
arrived and ask while we have already received. Then,
indeed, we can comfort each other with the words of
Paul.

There is no need to worry; but if there is anything you
need, pray for it, asking God for it with prayer and
thanksgiving, and that peace of God, which is so much
greater than we can understand, will guard your hearts
and your thoughts, in Christ Jesus. (Philippians 4:6-7)

Chapter 9

COMMUNITY AND PRAYER

―――――――●⊱ ⊰●―――――――

Tabor and Gethsemane

The movement from illusion to prayer requires a gradual detachment from all false ties and an increasing surrender to him from whom all good things come. It takes courage to move away from the safe place into the unknown, even when we know that the safe place offers false safety and the unknown promises us a saving intimacy with God. We realize quite well that giving up the familiar and reaching out with open arms toward him who transcends all our mental grasping and clinging makes us very vulnerable. Somewhere we sense that although holding on to our illusions might lead to a truncated life, the surrender in love leads to the cross. Jesus' way was the way of love but also the way of suffering. To Peter he said:

> . . . when you were young you put on your own belt and walked where you liked; but when you grow old you will stretch out your hands, and somebody else will put a belt round you and take you where you would rather not go. (John 21:18)

It is a sign of spiritual maturity when we can give up our illusory self-control and stretch out our hands to

God. But it would be just another illusion to believe that reaching out to God will free us from pain and suffering. Often, indeed, it will take us where we rather would not go. But we know that without going there we will not find our life. ". . . anyone who loses his life . . . will find it" (Matthew 16:25), Jesus says, reminding us that love is purified in pain.

Prayer, therefore, is far from sweet and easy. Being the expression of our greatest love, it does not keep pain away from us. Instead, it makes us suffer more since our love for God is a love for a suffering God and our entering into God's intimacy is an entering into the intimacy where all of human suffering is embraced in divine compassion. To the degree that our prayer has become the prayer of our heart we will love more and suffer more, we will see more light and more darkness, more grace and more sin, more of God and more of humanity. To the degree that we have descended into our heart and reached out to God from there, solitude can speak to solitude, deep to deep and heart to heart. It is there where love and pain are found together.

On two occasions, Jesus invited his closest friends, Peter, John and James, to share in his most intimate prayer. The first time he took them to the top of Mount Tabor, and there they saw his face shining like the sun and his clothes white as light (Matthew 17:2). The second time he took them to the garden of Gethsemane, and there they saw his face in anguish and his sweat falling to the ground like great drops of blood (Luke 22:44). The prayer of our heart brings us both to Tabor and Gethsemane. When we have seen God in his glory we will also see him in his misery, and when we have felt the ugliness of his humiliation we also will experience the beauty of his transfiguration.

The Hesychasts have always been very much aware of

these two inseparable aspects of prayer. While they usually stress detachment in prayer, they do not hesitate to compare the height of prayer with the illumination of Moses on Mount Sinai and with the transfiguration of Jesus on Mount Tabor. Theophan the Recluse writes:

> He who has repented travels towards the Lord. The way to God is an inner journey accomplished in the mind and heart. It is necessary so to attune the thoughts of the mind and the disposition of the heart that the spirit of man will always be with the Lord, as if joined with Him. He who is thus attuned is constantly enlightened by inner light, and receives in himself the rays of spiritual radiance . . . like Moses, whose face was glorified on the Mount because he was illumined by God.[1]

While waiting patiently in expectation is the foundation of the spiritual life, we also know that this waiting is full of joy since in prayer we already see the glory of him we are waiting for.

The Community of Faith

Much that has been said about prayer thus far might create the false impression that prayer is a private, individualistic and nearly secret affair, so personal and so deeply hidden in our inner life that it can hardly be talked about, even less be shared. The opposite is true. Just because prayer is so personal and arises from the center of our life, it is to be shared with others. Just because prayer is the most precious expression of being human, it needs the constant support and protection of the community to grow and flower. Just because prayer is our highest vocation needing careful attention and faithful perseverance, we cannot allow it to be a private affair. Just because prayer asks for a patient waiting in expectation, it should never become the most individualistic expression of the most individualistic emotion, but should always remain embedded in the life of the community of which we are part.

Prayer as a hopeful and joyful waiting for God is a really unhuman or superhuman task unless we realize that we do not have to wait alone. In the community of faith we can find the climate and the support to sustain and deepen our prayer and we are enabled to constantly look forward beyond our immediate and often narrowing private needs. The community of faith offers the protective boundaries within which we can listen to our deepest longings, not to indulge in morbid introspection, but to find our God to whom they point. In the community of faith we can listen to our feelings of loneliness, to our desires for an embrace or a kiss, to our sexual urges, to our cravings for sympathy, compassion or just a good word; also to our search for insight and to our hope for companionship and friendship. In the community of faith we can listen to all these longings and find the courage, not to avoid them or cover them up, but to confront them in order to discern God's presence in their midst. There we can affirm each other in our waiting and also in the realization that in the center of our waiting the first intimacy with God is found. There we can be patiently together and let the suffering of each day convert our illusions into the prayer of a contrite people. The community of faith is indeed the climate and source of all prayer.

A People Fashioned by God

The word "community" usually refers to a way of being together that gives us a sense of belonging. Often students complain that they do not experience much community in their school; ministers and priests wonder how they can create a better community in their parishes; and social workers, overwhelmed by the alienating influences of modern life, try hard to form communities in the neighborhood they are working in. In all these situations the word "community" points to a way of togetherness in which people can experience themselves as a meaningful part of a larger group.

Although we can say the same about the Christian community, it is important to remember that the Christian community is a waiting community, that is, a community which not only creates a sense of belonging but also a sense of estrangement. In the Christian community we say to each other, "We are together, but we cannot fulfill each other . . . we help each other, but we also have to remind each other that our destiny is beyond our togetherness." The support of the Christian community is a support in common expectation. That requires a constant criticism of anyone who makes the community into a safe shelter or a cozy clique, and a constant encouragement to look forward to what is to come.

The basis of the Christian community is not the family tie, or social or economic equality, or shared oppression or complaint, or mutual attraction . . . but the divine call. The Christian community is not the result of human efforts. God has made us into his people by calling us out of "Egypt" to the "New Land," out of the desert to fertile ground, out of slavery to freedom, out of our sin to salvation, out of captivity to liberation. All these words and images give expression to the fact that the initiative belongs to God and that he is the source of our new life together. By our common call to the New Jerusalem, we recognize each other on the road as brothers and sisters. Therefore, as the people of God, we are called *ekklesia* (from the Greek *kaleo* = call; and *ek* = out), the community called out of the old world into the new.

Since our desire to break the chains of our alienation is very strong today, it is of special importance to remind each other that, as members of the Christian community, we are not primarily for each other but for God. Our eyes should not remain fixed on each other but be directed forward to what is dawning on the horizon of our existence. We discover each other by following the same vocation and by supporting each other in the same search. Therefore, the Christian community is not a closed circle of people embracing each other, but a forward-moving group of companions bound together by the same voice asking for their attention.

It is quite understandable that in our large anonymous cities we look for people on our "wave length" to form small communities. Prayer groups, Bible-study clubs and house-churches all are ways of restoring or deepening our awareness of belonging to the people of God. But sometimes a false type of like-mindedness can narrow our sense of community. We all should have the mind of Jesus Christ, but we do not all have to have the mind of a school teacher, a carpenter, a bank director, a congressman or whatever socioeconomic or political group. There is a great wisdom hidden in the old bell tower calling people with very different backgrounds away from their homes to form one body in Jesus Christ. It is precisely by transcending the many individual differences that we can become witnesses of God who allows his light to shine upon poor and rich, healthy and sick alike. But it is also in this encounter on the way to God that we become aware of our neighbor's needs and begin to heal each other's wounds.

During the last few years I was part of a small group of students who regularly celebrated the Eucharist together. We felt very comfortable with each other and had found "our own way." The songs we sang, the words we used, the greetings we exchanged all seemed quite natural and spontaneous. But when a few new students joined us, we discovered that we expected them to follow our way and go along with "the way we do things here." We had to face the fact that we had become clannish, substituting our minds for the mind of Jesus Christ. Then we found out how hard it is to give up familiar ways and create space for the strangers, to make a new common prayer possible.

Not without reason the Church is called a "pilgrim church," always moving forward. The temptation to settle in a comfortable oasis, however, has often been too great to resist and frequently the divine call is forgotten and unity broken. At those times not just individuals but whole groups are caught in the illusion of safety, and prayer is shriveled into a partisan affair.

This explains why ideas, concepts and techniques developed and used in contemporary groups cannot be transposed without careful consideration to the Christian community. When we describe the ideal Christian community as a "happy family" or as a "group of very sensitive people" or as an "action or pressure group," we only speak about a secondary and often temporary trait. Although it might be helpful to incorporate into the life of the Christian community behavior patterns and techniques which are derived from other forms of group life, we will have to relativize these attempts by making them subservient to the self-understanding of the Christian community as a people fashioned by God. Many interpersonal processes, leadership patterns and strategies that have been identified by psychological and sociological studies of groups can indeed offer new insight in the understanding of the life of the Christian community. But the unique nature of the Christian community requires a constant awareness of the limited applicability of these findings. While living between the first and second coming of the Lord, the Christian community finds its meaning in a patient waiting in expectation for the time in which God will be all in all. The community of faith always points beyond itself and speaks its own unique language, which is the language of prayer.

The Language of the Community

Prayer is the language of the Christian community. In prayer the nature of the community becomes visible because in prayer we direct ourselves to the one who forms the community. We do not pray to each other, but together we pray to God, who calls us and makes us into a new people. Praying is not one of the many things the community does. Rather, it is its very being. Many discussions about prayer do not take this very seriously. Sometimes it seems as if the Christian community is "so busy" with its projects and plans that there is neither the time nor the mood to pray. But when prayer is no longer its primary concern, and when its many activities are no longer seen and experienced as part of prayer itself, the community quickly degenerates into a club with a common cause but no common vocation.

By prayer, community is created as well as expressed. Prayer is first of all the realization of God's presence in the midst of his people and, therefore, the realization of the community itself. Most clear and most noticeable are the words, the gestures and the silence through which the community is formed. When we listen to the word, we not only receive insight into God's saving work, but we also experience a new mutual bond. When we stand around the altar, eat bread and drink wine, kneel in meditation, or walk in procession we not only remember God's work in human history, but we also become aware of his creative presence here and now. When we sit together in silent prayer, we create a space where we sense that the one we are waiting for is already touching us, as he touched Elijah standing in front of the cave (1 Kings 19:13).

But the same words, gestures and silence are also the ways in which the community reaches out to the one it is waiting for. The words we use are words of longing. The little piece of bread we eat and the little portion of wine we drink make us aware of our most profound hunger and thirst, and the silence deepens our sensitivity to the calling voice of God. Therefore, the prayer of the community is also the expression of its unfulfillment and desire to reach the house of God. Thus the praying community celebrates God's presence while waiting, and affirms his absence while recognizing that he is already in its midst. Thus God's presence becomes a sign of hope and his absence a call for penance.

Prayer as the language of the community is like our mother tongue. Just as a child learns to speak from his parents, brothers, sisters and friends but still develops his own unique way of expressing himself, so also our individual prayer life develops by the care of the praying community. Sometimes it is hard to point to any specific organizational structure which we can call "our community." Our community is often a very intangible reality made up of people, living as well as dead, present as well as absent, close as well as distant, old as well as young. But without some form of community individual prayer cannot be born or developed. Communal and individual prayer belong together as two folded hands. Without community, individual prayer easily degenerates into egocentric and eccentric behavior, but without individual prayer, the prayer of the community quickly becomes a meaningless routine. Individual and community prayer cannot be separated without harm. This explains why spiritual leaders tend to be very critical of those who want to isolate themselves and why they stress the importance of continuing ties with a larger community where individual prayer can be guided. This also explains why the same leaders have always encouraged the individual member of their communities to spend time and energy in personal prayer, realizing as they do that community alone can never fulfill the desire for the most unique intimate relationship between a human being and his or her God.

Until the Last Day

The prayer of our heart can grow strong and deep within the boundaries of the community of faith. The community of faith, strengthened in love by our individual prayers, can lift them up as a sign of hope in common praise and thanksgiving. Together we reach out to God beyond our many individual limitations while offering each other the space for our own most personal search. We may be very different people with different nationalities, colors, histories, characters and aspirations, but God has called all of us away from the darkness of our illusions into the light of his glory. This common call transforms our world into the place where Gethsemane and Tabor both can exist, our time into the time of patient but joyful waiting for the last day, and ourselves into each other's brothers and sisters. St. Paul encourages us to be faithful to this common call when he writes:

. . . you know very well that the Day of the Lord is going to come like a thief in the night. . . . But it is not as if you live in the dark, my brothers, for that Day to overtake you like a thief. No, you are all sons of light and sons of the day: we do not belong to the night or to darkness, so we should not go on sleeping, as everyone else does, but stay wide awake and sober. . . . Let us put on faith and love for a breastplate, and the hope of salvation for a helmet. God . . . meant us . . . to win salvation through our Lord Jesus Christ, who died for us so that, alive or dead, we should still live united to him. So give encouragement to one another, and keep strengthening one another . . ." (1 Thessalonians 5:2–11)

When we reach out to God individually as well as in community, constantly casting off the illusions that keep us captive, we can enter into the intimate union with him while still waiting for the day of his final return. Then the words of the old pilgrim song become our words:

> I lift my eyes to the mountains:
> where is help to come from?
> Help comes to me from Yahweh,
> who made heaven and earth.
>
> No letting our footsteps slip!
> This guard of yours, he does not doze!
> The guardian of Israel
> does not doze or sleep.
>
> Yahweh guards you, shades you.
> With Yahweh at your right hand
> sun cannot strike you down by day,
> nor moon at night.

Yahweh guards you from harm,
he guards your lives,
he guards you leaving, coming back,
now and for always.
(Psalm 121)

CONCLUSION

On the night before his death, Jesus said to his apostles:

> In a short time you will no longer see me, and then a short time later you will see me again. . . . I tell you . . . you will be weeping and wailing while the world will rejoice; you will be sorrowful, but your sorrow will turn to joy. . . . you are sad now, but I shall see you again, and your hearts will be full of joy, and that joy no one shall take from you. (John 16:16–22)

We are living in this short time, a time, indeed, full of sadness and sorrow. To live this short time in the spirit of Jesus Christ, means to reach out from the midst of our pains and to let them be turned into joy by the love of him who came within our reach. We do not have to deny or avoid our loneliness, our hostilities and illusions. To the contrary: When we have the courage to let these realities come to our full attention, understand them and confess them, then they can slowly be converted into solitude, hospitality and prayer. This does not imply that a mature spiritual life is a life in which our old lonely hostile self with all its illusions simply disappears and we live in complete serenity with a peaceful mind and a pure heart. Just as our adulthood shows the marks of the struggles of our youth, so our solitude bears the signs of lonely hours, our care for others reflects at times angry feelings and our prayer sometimes reveals the memory and the presence of many illusions. Transformed in love, however, these painful signs become signs of hope, as the wounds of Jesus did for the doubting Thomas.

Once God has touched us in the midst of our struggles and has created in us the burning desire to be forever united with him, we will find the courage and the confidence to prepare his way and to invite all who share our life to wait with us during this short time for the day of complete joy. With this new courage and new confidence we can strengthen each other with the hopeful words of Paul to Titus:

. . . God's grace has been revealed, and it has made salvation possible for the whole human race and taught us that what we have to do is to give up everything that does not lead to God, and all our worldly ambitions; we must be self-restrained and live good and religious lives here in this present world, while we are waiting in hope for the blessing which will come with the Appearing of the glory of our great God and Saviour Christ Jesus. (Titus 2:11–13)

NOTES

Foreword

1. *The Divine Comedy*, "Inferno," Canto I.
2. John Climacus, *The Ladder of Divine Ascent*, trans. by Lazarus Moore (New York: Harper, 1959), p. 203.

Chapter 1

1. *Newsweek*, January 15, 1973.
2. *Walden and Other Writings* (New York: Modern Library, 1937, 1950), pp. 723–24.
3. *The Prophet* (New York: Alfred A. Knopf, 1951), pp. 15–16.
4. *Zen Flesh, Zen Bones*, comp. by Paul Reps (Garden City, N.Y.: Doubleday, Anchor Books, 1961), pp. 30–31.

Chapter 2

1. *Letters to a Young Poet* (New York: Norton, 1954), pp. 18–19.
2. Ibid., pp. 34–35.
3. Ibid., pp. 46–47.
4. *Gift from the Sea*, Anne Morrow Lindbergh (New York: Pantheon Books, 1955), p. 40.
5. Ibid., p. 40.
6. *The Sign of Jonas* (Garden City, N.Y.: Doubleday, Image Books, 1956), p. 261.
7. *Conjectures of a Guilty Bystander* (Garden City, N.Y.: Doubleday, Image Books, 1968), pp. 157–58.
8. *Letters to a Young Poet*, p. 59.
9. *Gift from the Sea*, p. 40.
10. *The Prophet*, p. 50.

Chapter 3

1. *The Sign of Jonas,* p. 323.
2. *Contemplation in a World of Action* (Garden City, N.Y.: Doubleday, Image Books, 1973), p. 161.
3. Ibid., p. 165.

Chapter 4

1. *Walden,* p. 65.
2. See Castaneda, *A Separate Reality* (New York: Simon and Schuster, 1971), especially pp. 218–19.
3. *Zen Flesh, Zen Bones,* p. 5.

Chapter 6

1. *Poverty of Spirit* (New York: Newman Press, 1960), p. 45.

Chapter 7

1. New York *Times,* Sunday, August 11, 1974, Section 4, p. 18.
2. Regulae Breviter Tractatae, 296, II, 2.742C. See J. E. Bamberger, "MNHMH—DIATHESIS, The Psychic Dynamism in the Ascetical Theology of St. Basil," *Orientalia Christiana Periodica,* Vol. XXXIV, Fasc. II, 1968.
3. *The Art of Prayer,* comp. by Khariton (London: Faber and Faber, 1966), p. 119.
4. *New Seeds of Contemplation* (New York: New Directions, 1961), p. 159.
5. *First and Last Notebooks* (New York: Oxford, 1970), p. 99.

Chapter 8

1. *Confessions of St. Augustine,* trans. by F. J. Sheed (New York: Sheed and Ward, 1943), p. 178.
2. *The Way of a Pilgrim,* trans. from the Russian by R. M. French (New York: Seabury Press, 1965).
3. Introduction, *The Art of Prayer,* p. 9.
4. *The Way of a Pilgrim,* p. 10.
5. Ibid., p. 16.

6. Ibid., p. 17–18.
7. Ibid., p. 18.
8. *The Way of a Pilgrim,* p. 19.
9. Ibid., pp. 19–20.
10. *Franny and Zooey* (Boston: Little, Brown, 1961).
11. *The Art of Prayer,* p. 110.
12. See Anthony Bloom, *Living Prayer* (Springfield, Ill.: Templegate, 1966); *Beginning to Pray* (New York: Paulist Press, 1970); *Courage to Pray* (New York: Paulist Press, 1973).
13. *The Art of Prayer,* p. 110.

Chapter 9

1. *The Art of Prayer,* p. 73.